ACKNOWLEDGEM

Produced with the support and generosity of the Plett Founda

Many of the Mennonite heritage images are from the author's ....al collection along with family archives.

Special thanks to Graham Schellenberg from the Neubergthal Commons Museum for the contribution of Mennonite heritage photos. Also, thanks to Marg Hein Wiebe for the contribution of Mennonite heritage photos.

Thanks to my granddaughters Hailey Sayers (Kreksconaitis) for editing and design, and also to Kahla Yzerman for coverage page design.

Thanks to Catherine McGregor for the sketch of the children's Christmas program.

All original oil paintings and food photography by author and artist Maria Klippenstein

Special Thanks to all the people who contributed to the Traditional Mennonite Heritage recipes, past and present.

The author's moral rights have been asserted. All rights reserved. No part of this publication may be reproduced, stored in a retrieval system or transmitted in any form or by any means, electronic, mechanical, photocopying or otherwise, without permission of the publisher.

Faspa 2nd Edition

Copyrighted
All Rights Reserved ©

CONTENT

THE STORY

The cookbook is not only a book to be used for cooking, but it tells a story of a way of life and how as a small Mennonite girl, I lived, ate, grew and communicated with the wealth of family, neighbours, church and school in my traditional community.

Mennonites are social people, committed to true hospitality. We serve each other and abide by the household motto "Love God and Love your Neighbour as Yourself." If you don't have you are given and if you have you give. We are our brother's keeper in the Mennonite community and to the world community.

The Mennonites are a passive culture and do not believe in taking revenge, taking up arms, or fighting of any kind but live true to the anabaptist traditions of servitude, humility and love.
I was born into an orthodox Mennonite family whose roots originated from the Netherlands, Germany and Russia. In 1874, fearing persecution, my family fled to Canada from Chortitza Russia, along with the families of the Chortitze Mennonite Church community. A large migration of Mennonites fled in 1874 to take up land to farm, starting a colony in Southern Manitoba.

Due to political and religious persecution, orthodox Mennonites were willing to leave all their wealth and possessions to survive the cultural genocide of Mennonite people in Russia. The migration of 1874 was the beginning of the Mennonite Heritage and Traditions in Canada. Today, there are traditional Mennonite churches throughout North and South America, as well as heritage sites, museums, festivals and other celebrations of this unique and humble culture.

THE AUTHOR

My name is Maria Klippenstein (born Neufeld). I was born in Steinbach Manitoba on September 25th, 1940. My parents were Suzanna and Gerhard Neufeld.

My parents lived with my mother's parents Jacob and Maria Hiebert in their big home and farm. My first 4 years of life are filled with the memories of this homestead and formed a significant part of my upbringing in this faith and tradition I have spent my life preserving.

After leaving the homestead, my parents carried on with the Mennonite way of life. I grew up only speaking Plautdietsch – a dialect of low German specific to Mennonites.

We were members of an orthodox Mennonite Chortitzer Church and followed their religious tradition and teachings.

I was married in the Chortitzer Church in the village of Chortitze, Manitoba to John Klippenstein, his family also were of the same faith and traditions. I have strived my whole life to value, pass on and preserve the cultural heritage of a persecuted people, the Mennonites.

FASPA

Faspa is a Traditional meal that is served in a Mennonite home, it is served in the afternoon around 3 o'clock. The Faspa meal is a time during the week for a break from your work.

Faspa on Sundays is a special time for family and friends to gather, share food, and visit. These Sunday Faspa visits were usually by invitation, but it wasn't uncommon to also have friends and family drop by for a Sunday Faspa visit.

Sunday Faspa was traditionally shared at the family home. The tradition was to always be prepared for visits and have the fixings ready for the meal.

A traditional Faspa meal is homemade zwieback, jams, cheese from the local cheese factory, home canned dills, and canned fruit preserves. Cakes and cookies were also a must and were baked on Saturday in preparation for the Sunday Faspa.

Faspa was typically served with a good cup of coffee, thick fresh cream for the coffee, and some sugar cubes for dunking in the coffee. Coffee was served together with the bread and cheese.

The table settings for Faspa were important. When preparing the table, you brought out your best linens and china.

All Mennonites served this traditional meal and participated in these traditions.

THE MENNONITES WHO ARE THEY?

The Mennonites were organized as a church in Zurich, Switzerland in 1525, calling themselves The Brethren. In 1536 Menno Simon became a member of the Brethren Church. Because of Menno Simon's leadership and great ministry, the Brethren were soon referred to as the Mennonites. Eventually the Brethren adopted and called themselves Mennonites.

The Mennonites in 1525 studied scripture and believed in the teachings of Jesus Christ. Their main belief and practise were to follow in the footsteps of Christ and his teachings in their everyday life and worship. They believed in and practiced only adult baptism. Furthermore, their whole religion and belief was based also in a nonviolence and pacifism practise. It was to love your neighbour as yourself and to do no harm to anybody. It was to practise to care for your fellow man and with a non-aggressive approach. They also adhered to the Law of Moses and the commandments.

"So, to be in the world but not part of the world" in attitudes and deeds.
Through the years of 1525 - 1874 and beyond the Mennonites suffered great persecution, because of their Religious beliefs and for their nonviolent lifestyle.

"There is some parallel between the term Mennonite and a Jew"

They were a group of people that had a common belief and suffered great persecution because of it. This, therefore created an ethnic and a cultural identity. From about 1530 – 1917, about 400 years, the Mennonites of Danzig, from different parts of Europe and Russia were ethnically isolated due to the pressure of outside religions and cultures. Because of this isolation, the Mennonites developed into a separate people easily distinguishable by their Religion, language, dress, and way of life.

In order escape persecution, maintain, and practise their Religious freedom, the Mennonites had to relocate many times throughout Europe. Their last country of location mostly being Russia from 1786 - 1874 and others beyond.

By the year 1874 there was a large immigration from Russia coming to Canada and the Americas.

Many Mennonites from 1917 - 1940's, were severely persecuted in Russia. Many families and family members were killed and executed. Mennonites in Russia and elsewhere were killed, imprisoned, starved to death, and tortured because of their faith in God, Mennonite Religion and way of life.

Some families in Canada and the USA to this day do not know what happened to their loved ones in Russia or how they were killed.

The Mennonites were/are a plain humble people, conservative in their dress and their approach to life. God, Church and Family was/is of the utmost importance in their lives. Their spoken language was/is Plautdietsch, with more of the written word being in German. Children were taught both languages and were taught the written word in gothic German. All schools were ordained by the church and teachers were chosen accordingly.

The Mennonite Plautdietsch is still being spoken today, mostly by adults. It is a language that needs to be revived so other generations will become fluent to speak it and remember.
More learning books and dictionaries are being published.

Life in a Mennonite Community was in a way a communal life with people caring and helping each other when needed. Nobody was left behind or neglected in time of need, especially women and children who might have lost the head of the house in sickness or death. The WAISENAMT was created to help widows and orphans. This was a Mennonite Financial Institution created to help the Mennonites in need. "Do not merely look after your own personal interest, but also for the interests of others" Philippians 2:4 was the teaching of obedience for a Mennonite.

Most of the hard work that was required to be done on the farm or elsewhere in the Mennonite community was done as a group. Not only did the Mennonites help each other out financially but they always helped out in work and labour without charge.

From 1525 throughout Europe, Baltic, Netherlands, Germany and Russia the Mennonites were very successful in their farming, manufacturing and artistic endeavours. They were very hard working, innovative and dedicated people. Very often when they were forced to relocate, they had to settle in the worst of land or some swamp land. Within a short period of time it would be developed into a "Garden of Eden" per say.

" The psychology toward the Mennonite seems to have been the same as to the Jew" both were needed and feared.

The Mennonites mostly developed small villages for themselves to live in with each village having a centre street. Each family property having a home place and yard and garden facing the street in the village. The land for pasture land, hay and grain was further outside the villages. In time because of all the relocations to different countries in Europe, also the Baltics the Mennonites created an interesting and unique Architectural style. Which they recreated in all different countries they came to. Most interesting styles such as the House barn, the different although plain different window shutters, smoke houses, summer kitchens and unique ovens to heat homes and cook. Many of these Architectural designs were also recreated here in Canada. The book Architectural Heritage a book on Mennonite traditional architecture shows and features many examples.
Because the Mennonites had to make many relocations to protect their Religion and escape persecution throughout Europe, Germany, Baltic and Russia they developed a unique culinary style.

The Mennonite Religious History and Ethnic Traditions developed into a Heritage that continues in their culinary food. Every person who at one time or who still belongs to this Mennonite Ethnic group can relate to these tastes and this culinary style. They know and remember the food and some of the Traditions that come with the serving of certain Mennonite Heritage dishes. We can all relate to the foods we loved and ate, the desire for such tastes and smells never die.

FREISCHTIKJ...MEDDACH.FASPA. OVENKOST.NACHTKOST

This book FASPA is my contribution to my wonderful heritage of being born and still being a practising MENNONITE. FASPA is written and published to help Mennonites to remember and appreciate the heritage they have and came from.
This cookbook is also for others to better understand who Mennonites are and this includes all the recipes to cook those great dishes.

MENNONITE ARCHITECTURE HOUSEBARN
(Mennonite Homes and Barn)

Traditional Mennonite Architecture, Heritage Mennonite Housebarn and other structures. Circa 1874 to 1935 in Southern Manitoba.

The Commons Barn formerly known as the Klippenstein Barn "Is in the Family a Great Uncle" is located at Neubergthal Mennonite Village in Southern Manitoba.

The Neubergthal Mennonite Village is the best-preserved Mennonite Village in all North America. This restored and preserved Mennonite Village depicts the Mennonite way of life back to its roots in Europe and Russia. Neubergthal Village is a Canadian Historical Site

Traditional Mennonite Family Farm Homes in southern Manitoba Circa 1920.Pictured here with growing families.

Families dressed in traditional Mennonite dress.

Original oil painting on canvas by Maria Klippenstein

The home and farm of Grandmother Louise Dueck in Southern Manitoba

MENNONITE HERITAGE
FAMILY PHOTO

Jacob and Katherina Hiebert

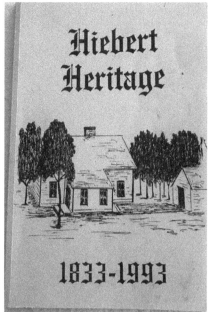

My Great Grandparents...
Jacob Hiebert and Katherina Hiebert were born in Russia and came to Canada in 1874 and settled in southern Manitoba.

Jacob Hiebert b. 1833 - d. 1906   Katherina Hiebert b. 1855 - d. 1916.

Katherina was a very well-known midwife and largely a self-taught country doctor in southern Manitoba. She learned her knowledge in medicine and healing from medical books she acquired from Germany and the United States. The vast amount of knowledge she had and practiced, was directly learned from the native aboriginal women in the southern Manitoba area.

Katherina was an expert herbalist and medicine maker for healing. She would scour the forests and meadows to collect "Swedish bitters", chamomile, thyme and more. She had learned about many of these herbs and methods for cure from her 4 months stay at the native village while being cured herself by the native women of a large breast cancer growth.

Katherina pictured here in the traditional dress in the prayer cap of the Chortitzer Church.

Grandparents: Jacob H Hiebert b.1889-d.1952 - Katherina Maria D Hiebert b.1888-d.1982
Many of the Mennonite Traditional recipes in this book come from Maria Hiebert.

My parents:

Gerhard H Neufeld b. 1917 - d. 1976
Suzanna H. Neufeld b. 1919 - d. 2001

Suzanna was very good chef and cook.
Many of her recipes are featured in this book.

BREADS & ROLLS

ORGANIC GRAIN BROWN BREAD

4 Cups of warm water
2 cups of organic mixed grains and bran
3 Eggs
¼ cup molasses
½ Tbsp. salt
6 – 7 cups of flour or enough to make soft but firm dough
6 Tbsp. melted butter or olive oil
<u>Yeast Mixture:</u> dissolve the yeast and sugar in warm water
3 Tbsp. yeast
 ½ cup warm water
3 Tsp. Sugar.
This is one batch for the kitchen aid, one batch makes three loaves.
Add the water, yeast mixture, the grains, molasses, eggs, salt and some of the flour into kitchen aid bowl. Turn machine on to very slow and mix the flour add more flour into mixture until you have soft but firm dough. Keep machine running and drizzle butter or oil until you have smooth dough. Place in large dough bowel let rise in warm place until double in bulk. Make into loaves, let rise in warm place covered with cloth and then a plastic sheet till double. Bake at 350-375 till brown, 20-30 min.
<u>Grain Mixture:</u>
Buy in bulk Organic 7-grains mix, flax seed, sunflower seeds (unroasted & unsalted) wheat bulgur, wheat bran, oat bran or other grains preferred. Mix all grains – the 7 grain and the bran in larger volume.

Recipe created by Maria Klippenstein

BROWN BREAD LOAVES

Milk Mixture: heat milk, honey and butter and water, then cool to lukewarm
1 Cup milk
1 Tbsp. liquid honey
½ Cup butter
1 ½Cups water (potato water)
Yeast Mixture: dissolve: the yeast and sugar in warm water
2 Tsp. sugar
2 Tbsp. yeast
½ cup warm water
Dry ingredients:
4 Cups whole wheat flour
3 Tsp. salt
½ Cup soy flour
½ Cup wheat germ
½ Cup sesame seeds
½ Cup wheat bran
1 – 1 ½ Cup all-purpose flour
Add yeast mixture to cooled milk mixture and 2 cups of the whole wheat flour.
Beat with wooden spoon to combine. Add in remaining dry ingredients and knead to make smooth firm dough. Let rise, punch down. Let rise again, make into loaves. Let rise, then bake in moderate oven at 350 for 20 – 30 min.

WHITE BREAD BUNS

4 Cups warm water
1 Tbsp. Salt
3 Eggs (optional)
Yeast Mixture: dissolve the yeast and sugar in warm water
3 Tbsp. yeast
½ cup warm water
3 Tbsp. sugar
Other Ingredients:
6 Tbsp. melted butter or lard or olive oil
8 – 10 cups of all-purpose flour
In the kitchen aid bowl with dough hook attached add the water, yeast mixture and salt. Also add 1 or 2 cups of the flour turn on machine to very slow, and then keep adding the rest of the flour till you have soft but firm dough. With machine still running, begin to drizzle the melted butter or olive oil to the dough to make smooth dough.
Place dough in large dough bowl and let rise in warm place till double in bulk. Punch down and let rise again till double in bulk. Make buns and place in pans, let rise covered with cloth and plastic sheet or let cold rise uncovered on counter till double in bulk. Bake in moderate oven 350 – 375 till golden brown about 15 minutes.
One batch will make about 2 ½ dozen buns.

Recipe created by Maria Klippenstein

MENNONITE ZWEIBACK

Milk Mixture: scald milk, cream, sugar and salt then cool to lukewarm.
1 ½ Cup Milk
1 Cup Cream
½ Cup Sugar
1 Tsp. salt
Yeast Mixture:
Dissolve the yeast and sugar in warm water
3 Tbsp. Yeast
1 Tsp. Sugar
½ Cup Water (warm)
Other Ingredients:
1 ½ Cups Potato Water
3 Eggs
½ - ¾ Cups Melted Butter
8 – 10 Cups of Flour (or enough flour to make soft but firm dough)
This recipe is for one batch in Kitchen Aid repeat for more bread and mix batches in bread bowl.
For potato water:
Peel 2 small potatoes, cut fine and put in small pot covered with enough water for the recipe about 2 cups.
Bring to boil and cook till potatoes cooked soft. Cool to lukewarm.

Mix eggs, luke warm potato water together into the kitchen aid bowl. Add luke warm milk mixture and yeast mixture
Add some of the flour and slowly start machine. Keep adding flour and the melted butter until dough is smooth, soft, but firm.
Place dough in large bread bowl and let rise in warm place until double in bulk. Punch down and let rise again.
Set buns on baking trays. To make the traditional buns make as follows:
Make one larger bun then on top of the larger bun place a smaller bun and with two front fingers press the top bun into larger bun. Let rise covered with a soft cloth and top over with a plastic sheet let rise till double in bulk.
Bake in moderate hot oven 350 till brown.

This is a very old Traditional Mennonite Heritage bread recipe, baked for special occasions such as weddings and funerals.

When these buns were served at a wedding or funeral, they were served with some sugar cubes on the side. Tradition was that you dipped the sugar cube in your coffee or tea and ate it together with the bun

WHITE BREAD BUNS OR LOAVES

8 Cups warm water (substitute part with potato water)

1 Cup soft lard

½ Cup soft butter

2 Tbsp. salt

All-purpose flour (enough to make soft but firm dough)

<u>Yeast Mixture:</u> dissolve the yeast and sugar in warm water

4 Tbsp. yeast

2 Tsp. sugar

½ Cup warm water.

In large bread bowl add water, yeast mixture, some of the flour to make thin paste. Let sit till bubbly then stir in salt, soft lard and butter. Leave some of the butter to grease bowl and dough. Keep adding flour and keep kneading, adding flour and kneading till dough is soft but smooth. Grease bowl and dough. Let rise till double in bulk, punch down and let rise again. Set buns on baking sheets or make loaves in loaf pans. Let rise till double. Bake in 350 – 375 oven till golden brown.

Recipe: Created by Susan Neufeld, Maria Klippenstein's mom. This was her daily recipe for her bread she made every week to nourish her family

BRAIDED EGG BREAD

2 Cups warm water
3 Eggs (beaten)
¼ cup butter or oil
3 Tbsp. sugar
½ Tsp. saffron (optional)
6 Cups all purpose flour
1 Tbsp. salt
Yeast Mixture: dissolve the yeast and sugar in warm water

3 Tbsp. Yeast
2 Tsp. sugar
½ Cup warm water
Add yeast and sugar to warm water till dissolved.
Into large bread bowl add the flour, sugar, saffron and salt. Make a well in centre of the flour add the water, eggs, butter and the yeast mixture. Work the flour to make a soft and knead till smooth. Grease bowl and let rise till double in bulk. Punch down and divide into 2 parts. Cut each piece into three parts. Roll each piece until a longer cylinder is formed. Lay the three cylinders side by side and loosely braid dough to form braided loaf, tuck ends under. Place on greased flat baking sheet. Brush tops with milk and egg wash. Sprinkle tops with sesame seed or poppy seed. Let rise till double. Bake in a 400-degree oven for 15 min. Reduce heat to 375 and bake about another 30 min.
French glaze: 1 egg yolk mixed with milk, brush on dough before rising.

A favourite for holiday baking

PEPANATE PEPPERNUTS (soft)

Scald: the milk, cream, sugar, salt and butter. Cool to lukewarm
1 cup milk
¾ cup butter
 ½ cup sugar
1 Tsp. salt
Dissolve: the yeast and sugar in warm potato water, then add to lukewarm milk mixture
4 Tsp. yeast
2 Tsp. sugar
½ cup warm potato water
Add:
1 cup mashed potatoes (lukewarm)
2 eggs (well beaten)
1 ½ Tsp. black pepper
1 Tsp. ground anise
2 Tsp. ground cinnamon
4 cups flour – enough flour to make soft dough
Knead till dough is soft and smooth. Let rise till double in bulk (covered) in a warm place. When double in bulk-punch down. Make into small buns, 2 ½ in balls roll in fine sugar and set in greased baking sheet. Let rise until double in bulk-in warm place. Bake in moderate oven 350 – 375 till light brown 10 – 12 min.

This is a Traditional Mennonite Heritage recipe baked for Christmas

HOT CROSS BUNS

Use dough recipe for the soft peppernuts recipe in this book.
When preparing the dough add the following with the liquids and flour before kneading.
1 ½ Cups raisins or currants
1 Cup of candied citrus (orange and lemon)
1 Tbsp. orange rind (finely chopped)
1 Tbsp. lemon rind (finely chopped)
1 Tsp. allspice
½ Tsp. nutmeg
½ Tsp. cloves
Add:
3 Tsp. cinnamon (total of)
2 ½ Tsp. pepper (total of)
(Do not add the anise) as to the peppernut recipe.
Let rise until double in bulk. Make into small buns, roll in sugar and place in greased pan, let rise in warm place until double.
Bake in 350 oven until golden brown.
When cool Ice with a cross design.

Adapted by Maria Klippenstein

LEMON BUNS

1 package lemon pie filling (cooked according directions) cooled.

Scald: the milk, sugar, salt and butter. Cool to lukewarm

1 Cup Milk

½ - ¾ Cup Butter

¼ Tsp. Salt

½ Cup Sugar

Add 4 Tbsp. Instant Yeast to lukewarm milk mixture and dissolve.

Beat 4 Eggs and add beaten eggs to milk mixture.

Add enough flour to make very soft dough. Knead till smooth.

Let rise in warm place cover until double in bulk. Roll out, cut into 4-inch squares. Cut slit in corner of square. Put cooled lemon pie filling in centre of square (about 1 Tsp.). Pull opposite corner through slit. Place in baking sheet. Let rise about 1 hour. Bake 350 for 5 – 10 minutes until light brown. Do not over bake drizzle icing on when buns are still very hot.

ICING

1 cup icing sugar

 Enough cream to make very thin icing.

1 Tsp. almond extract

Mix and use

PORTZELKY (NEW YEAR COOKIES)

<u>Scald:</u> the milk, cream, sugar, salt and butter. Cool to lukewarm
2 Cups milk
1 Cup cream
½ Cup sugar
½ Tsp. salt
4 Tbsp. butter
<u>Dissolve:</u> the yeast and sugar in warm water.
3 Tbsp. of yeast
2 Tsp. sugar
1 cup warm water
<u>Other Ingredients:</u>
8 Eggs well beaten
½ Tsp. ginger
¼ Tsp. nutmeg
1 Tsp. cinnamon
½ Tsp. ground cardamom (optional)
2 lbs of raisins
Mix all ingredients and add enough flour to make a stiff batter. Let rise till double in bulk. Drop by rounded tablespoon into hot, deep oil. Fry till golden brown and done. To serve: Put some portzelky in a plastic bag with some icing sugar and shake to cover with the dry icing.

This is a Traditional Mennonite Heritage recipe.
Recipe: created by Maria Klippenstein adapted from the Mennonite heritage recipe.

PASKA – EASTERBREAD

<u>Scald:</u> the milk, sugar, salt and butter. Cool to lukewarm

6 Cups whole milk

2 Cups sugar

½ Cup butter

2 Tsp. salt

<u>Dissolve:</u> the yeast and sugar in warm water.

¾ cup warm water

8 Tbsp. yeast

3 Tbsp. sugar

<u>Other Ingredients:</u>

12 Eggs

2 Oranges- the zest and juice

1 Lemon – the zest

3 Tbsp. cinnamon

3 Tbsp. pure vanilla

 1 1/2 – 3 Cups raisins

Flour for soft dough (all purpose)

Add yeast mixture to lukewarm milk mixture. Add beaten eggs, orange zest and juice, lemon zest, cinnamon, vanilla and raisins. Work in enough flour and knead for soft dough. Let rise until double in bulk.

Set paska dough into cylinder tube pans or large washed and well-greased juice tins.

Fill to 1/3 of the height of tin, let rise.

Bake at 325 – 350 degrees for 45 min. Remove from tins and cool on a rack in stand-up position. When cool ice top with thin icing letting the icing drip down the sides and sprinkle with colourful sprinkles.

To serve cut in rounds. Serve with following cheese spread.

<u>Cheese spread:</u>

Blend and mix

2 cups dry cottage cheese

2/3 cup cream cheese

1 Tbsp. lemon juice

 ½ cup icing sugar.

½ Tsp. lemon zest (optional)

Mix till smooth. Spread on sliced paska.

This is a Traditional Mennonite Heritage recipe served at Easter

CINNAMON BUNS

Scald: the milk, sugar, salt and butter. Cool to lukewarm

1 cup milk

½ cup sugar

1 ¼ Tsp. salt

6 Tbsp. butter

In large bowl or kitchen aid, beat 2 eggs, then add cooled mixture and add prepared yeast mixture.

Dissolve: the yeast and sugar in warm water:

3 Tbsp. of yeast

1 cup warm water

2 Tsp. sugar.

Add prepared yeast mixture to cooled milk mixture

Add enough flour to make soft dough. Place in greased bowl, brush with butter, then let rise until double in bulk in a warm place. Punch down and divide in two parts.

Roll out the parts and brush with ½ cup of melted butter. Sprinkle sugar mixture.

Sugar Mixture:

1 cup brown sugar

3 Tsp. cinnamon/ or as desired

Roll up and cut. Place in well-greased pan. Then brush generously with melted butter. Let rise. Bake in 350 oven for 8 – 10 minutes. Do not over bake, Frost when buns are hot with thin icing.

Icing: 1 cup icing sugar, cream and cream cheese to make thin icing. Add 1Tsp. almond extract.

Recipe from: Mrs. Maria Wiebe, Maria's aunt her father Gerhard Neufeld's sister.

GERMAN PANCAKES (PANKOUCKE)

5 Eggs
2 Cups whole milk, enough to make very thin pouring batter
½ Tsp. salt
4 Tsp. baking powder
6 Tbsp. melted butter
1 ½Cups flour
Flour to make very thin batter
In mixing bowl or kitchen aid add eggs, flour, baking powder and salt. Blend in milk for very thin batter and add melted butter. Pour very thin layer into hot skillet, lift and roll skillet to even out batter over the entire skillet. Batter should make very thin pancakes. Flip pancakes, when   done keep warm, stacked on converted dinner plate.
Serve with syrup or roll up and sprinkle with sugar.
Syrup:
1 Cup Brown sugar
2 Tbsp. water (approx.)
3 Tbsp. butter
1 Tsp. Maple flavour
Put sugar in pot with the water. Bring to boil for a few minutes. Take off heat add the butter and maple flavour. Serve hot. Or serve pancake with:
Cottage cheese filling in center of rolled pancake, topped with sour cream and frozen strawberries.

Recipe adapted by Maria from her mom's recipe Mrs. Susan Neufeld

POTATO PANCAKES

2 Medium Potato (shredded)
¼ Cup onion (chopped)
2 Eggs
¼ Cup cream
½ - ¾ Cup flour
1 Tsp. baking powder
Salt & pepper

Shred the potato and onion, place in bowl (can be pare cooked if desired and cooled). Add eggs, baking powder and flour and mix. Add salt and pepper to taste. Spoon a small ladle full on hot buttered skillet. Fry on both sides till done.
Serve with apple sauce and sour cream.

Recipe: Created by Maria Klippenstein.

CINNAMON TOAST

Cinnamon toast makes a great evening snack, with a cup of hot chocolate.
Bread slices – as many slices as desired for each person.
Generously butter bread slices on one side. Place bread slices into a cookie sheet, butter side up
Cinnamon and Sugar- mix ½ cup of sugar with 2 Tsp. of cinnamon mix well. Sprinkle sugar mixture evenly over the buttered bread. Sprinkle as much sugar mixture as desired.
Place cookie sheet with the cinnamon sugar bread slices under a pre-heated broil in oven.
Watch the bread under the broil and heat until butter and sugar melt. Do not burn.
Remove from oven and serve hot with hot cocoa.

Great treat for a bedtime snack for the children.
Created by Maria Klippenstein

WAFFLES AND VANILLA SAUCE

5 Eggs
2 Cups flour
4 Tsp. Baking powder
½ Tsp. Salt
¼ cup melted butter
Enough milk to make a medium batter. Beat eggs then add flour, baking powder, salt and melted butter. Mix and add enough milk to make a medium thin batter. Bake in waffle iron and serve with the warm vanilla sauce.

Vanilla Sauce:
2 Cups light cream or whole milk
¾ Cup sugar
Pinch of salt
2 Tbsp. butter
2 Tsp. pure vanilla
On heat in medium pot add cream, sugar and salt. When heated remove some of the liquid add flour, blend then add back into pot, stir and bring to a boil till thick. Take off heat, add butter and vanilla. Pour into serving pitcher and serve hot for the waffles. 4 Tbsp. flour or use part of batter to thicken sauce

This is a Traditional Mennonite Heritage recipe.

As a small girl, this treat was served in my grandmother's summer kitchen. The waffles were made with the old cast iron waffle maker that made heart shaped waffles on an open flame on the old wood burning cook stove. What a treat then, and what a treat for my grandchildren now

Recipe from: Maria Klippenstein's grandmother, Mrs. Maria Deorksen Hiebert.

DOUGHNUTS

<u>Scald:</u> the milk, sugar, and butter. Cool to lukewarm
1/2 Cup milk
1/2 Cup sugar
1/3 Cup butter
<u>Dissolve:</u> the yeast and sugar in warm water:
4 Tbsp. yeast
2 Tsp. sugar
1/2 Cup warm water
<u>Other Ingredients</u>
2 Eggs (well beaten)
1 Tsp. Vanilla
4 ½ Cups flour
Stir the eggs and vanilla into milk and yeast mixture. Gradually add flour knead dough until soft and smooth. Place dough in greased bowl and let rise until double in bulk, in warm place.
Punch down and roll out ½ inch thick. Cut with doughnut cutter and let rise till double. Then deep fry doughnuts in hot oil, until golden on both sides. Place in pan lined with paper towel. Then dip and coat with syrup.
SYRUP: In a pot add, 1 Cup sugar, ¼ Cup water, ¼ Cup butter.
Simmer 5 minutes then add 1 Tsp. vanilla.

Recipe: used by Maria Klippenstein as a teenager. She made these doughnuts for her family and friends. No Tim Horton's in those days.

ORANGE LOAF

<u>Scald:</u> the cream, sugar, and butter. Cool to lukewarm
2/3 Cups cream
2 Tbsp. sugar
¾ Cup butter
<u>Dissolve:</u> the yeast and sugar in warm water:
3 Tbsp. of yeast
1Tsp. sugar
½ cup warm water.
Let rise and add to lukewarm cream mixture.
<u>Other Ingredients:</u>
3 Eggs
4 ½ Cups flour
Beat eggs well add to cream and yeast mixture. Work in flour to mixture for soft dough, knead until smooth. Let rise until double in bulk.
Punch down, divide in 2 parts. Roll out and sprinkle with some of cinnamon sugar mixture, fold dough over roll out and sprinkle with cinnamon sugar mixture, repeat until ½ of sugar mixture is used. This will create the dough to layer. Repeat same with other ½ of dough.
<u>Cinnamon mixture:</u> 1 cup sugar and 3 Tsp. cinnamon
Put each piece in a 9"x9" pan. Let rise. Bake loafs at 350 for 15 min. Cover with the Syrup.

<u>Syrup:</u> 1 cup sugar, 1 ½ Tsp. orange rind, ¼ cup butter and ¼ cup orange juice.
Pour syrup over partially baked loaf, return to oven and bake 15 min more.

Recipe: from Maria Klippenstein's aunt Mrs. Leez Kehler, her mom's sister

FRIED BREAD

1 Cup warm water
2 Tbsp. sugar
1 Tbsp. yeast
3 Tbsp. melted butter
¼ Tsp. salt
Flour to make soft but firm dough
In bowl mix water, sugar and yeast. Let yeast dissolve, add some flour, the butter and salt. Knead and add more flour if needed till dough is soft but firm. Let rise till double in bulk. Roll out or pat out to about 2" thickness, cut into 3 – 4 in squares or any shape preferred, deep fry until golden brown.
Serve hot with jam and cheese.
Or
When still hot roll in a sugar and cinnamon mixture for a delicious treat.

On baking day in a Mennonite home when the bread was running low or it was all gone, you would take some of the bread dough and fry it to make nice hot fried bread for faspa and serve it with jam or sprinkled with sugar.

Recipe: created by Maria Klippenstein for her grandchildren who like the cinnamon treats sold at concession stands.

HOT BISCUTS (SCHNEJTKE)

3 cups all-purpose flour
½ cup hard butter (cut in chunks)
4 Tsp. baking powder
½ Tsp. baking soda
1 Tsp. salt
Milk, plain yogurt or buttermilk
Add flour, baking powder, baking soda and salt in bowl. Work in the hard butter but leave butter chunky. Add enough liquid from above to make soft, slightly sticky dough. Flour counter and pat out dough to about 1in. thick. Cut with 3in. round cutters. Place in pan, brush biscuits with milk or cream wash. Bake in 375 till golden.
Serve hot.

Recipe created by Maria Klippenstein a Mennonite staple when out of baked bread

BUBBAT

2 Cups flour
½ cup sugar
¼ Cup grape seed oil
4 Tsp. baking powder
½ Tsp. salt
2 Eggs
1 ½ Cup raisins, or optional (prunes or cranberries)
1 ½ cups whole milk & half cream
Mix dry ingredients, add raisins. Then add eggs, milk and cream. Put in loaf pan and bake at 350 till done. Serve warm with roasted chicken.
This also makes an excellent stuffing for chicken or duck put batter inside the chicken before baking or add during baking and continue to bake.

This is a Traditional Mennonite Heritage recipe.
Recipe: This recipe is from Mennonite Heritage cooking and adapted by Maria Klippenstein.

POPOVERS (FOR ROAST BEEF)

2 ½ cups whole milk
2 ½ cups flour
1 Tsp. coarse salt
6 eggs (slightly beaten)
Butter for pan
Heat oven to 425 degrees
Mix first three ingredients, then add eggs. Batter will be lumpy. Pre heat muffin tins until very hot. Brush with butter or put a little butter into each tin. Fill each tin a little over half full. Bake in oven until puffy and brown. Turn oven down and bake a little while longer. Serve with roast beef and gravy.

BROKKE

This is an old Traditional Mennonite Heritage recipe and was eaten for Faspa.
To have brokke for an individual serving:
Place a slice of bread in a small plate, sprinkle bread with 2-3 Tsp. of sugar or use your favourite jam. (Choke cherry jam was a Mennonite favourite)
Pour ¼ cup of hot coffee over the bread and top with 2 Tbsp. of heavy cream.
Use a Tsp. for serving and serve with some slices of cheese.

This is a Traditional Mennonite Heritage recipe.
This was Maria's father's Mr. Gerhard Neufeld favourite food for his Faspa.

ROLL KUCHEN

3 Eggs
¾ Cup milk
¼ Cup whipping cream
4 Tbsp. melted butter
Salt
Flour to make soft dough

Mix eggs, milk and cream. Mix in enough flour to make soft dough, then pour melted butter over dough and knead in. Cut dough into two pieces and roll out very thin, while rolling dough sprinkle salt and roll. Only use enough salt so top is slightly salted or to taste.

Then cut dough into 3inch x5inch pieces. Deep fry in deep hot oil, turn when light brown. Remove and drain on paper towel.

Kuchen should be puffed and flaky, great with Suma Borsht or watermelon.

This is a Traditional Mennonite Heritage recipe, and a favourite with everyone.

Recipe: Created by Maria's grandmother Maria Deorksen Hiebert

CHEESE HORN BUNS

Scald: milk, sugar, salt and butter. Cool to lukewarm.
1 Cup milk
2 Tbsp. Sugar
1 Tsp. salt
4 Tbsp. butter
Dissolve: yeast and sugar in warm water.
1 ½ Tbsp. yeast
1 Tsp. sugar
½ cup warm water.
Other Ingredients:
2 Eggs beaten
1 ½ Cups shredded cheddar cheese.
3 ½ - 4 cups all-purpose flour
In large bowl combine warm milk mixture and yeast mixture, add beaten eggs and cheese. Work in the flour, kneading until soft and smooth dough. Let rise till double in bulk. Make into buns, set unto greased baking sheet or set 3 small round buns into deeper muffin tin. Let rise till double. Bake at 325 ovens till golden brown.

BUTTER HORNS

1 – 500 ml Cottage cheese (dry curds)
1½ Cup butter
3 Cups flour
Cream cottage cheese till creamy. Mix butter to the cottage cheese and blend in the flour. Let stand in fridge overnight. Cut into squares and roll up. Bake in 400-degree oven until brown. Serve warm.

BANANA BREAD

½ Cup butter
1 Cup sugar
2 Eggs
3 Crushed bananas
2 Cups flour
1 Tsp. baking powder
¼ Tsp. salt
½ Cup cold coffee
1 Cup chopped mixed nuts
Mix in order given and pour into a greased loaf pan.
Bake 1 hr – 30 min at 350 degrees

Recipe: created by Mrs. Susan Neufeld

MARIA'S BANANA BREAD

1 Cup oil or ½ cup oil and ½ cup butter
2 Cups sugar (1 white and 1 brown)
2 Eggs
2 Cups mashed Bananas
2 Tsp. baking soda in 2 Tbsp. hot water
3 Cups flour
1 Tsp. cinnamon
1 Tsp. allspice
1 Tsp. salt
1 ½ Cup (walnuts, pecans) chopped
Mix in order given. Bake at 350 degrees in 2 loaf pans for 35 – 45 minutes.
Or until done and centre is firm.

Recipe created by Maria Klippenstein

CARROT BREAD

½ Cup oil
1 Cup sugar
2 Eggs
1 Cup shredded carrots
1 ½Cups flour
1 Tsp. baking powder
1 Tsp. baking soda
¼ Tsp. salt
1 Tsp. cinnamon
 ½ Cup milk
Nuts and raisins can be added if desired.
Mix in order given and pour into loaf pan.
Bake in oven at 350 for 55 min.

Recipe: Created by Mrs. Susan Neufeld

COOKIES & SLICES

OATMEAL COOKIES

1 Lb butter
3 Cups brown sugar
4 Eggs
2 Tsp. pure vanilla
Pinch of salt
6 – 5 Cups rolled oats (large flakes)
1½ Cup flour (scant)
4 Tsp. Baking powder
Mix and drop from spoon. Dough should be very soft. These cookies spread so leave room. Bake till slightly brown in moderate oven 350. About 8 minutes.
Put on rack to cool.
If desired add 1 cup less sugar and add 1 ½ cup semi-sweet pure chocolate chips

Recipe: Created by Maria's mom Mrs. Susan Neufeld

OATMEAL COOKIES

1 Cup butter
2 Cups brown sugar
2 Eggs
¼ Tsp. salt
2 Tsp. vanilla
2 Cups oatmeal (rolled oats)
1 Cup coconut (shredded) or 1 cup walnuts chopped
1 Tsp. baking soda
2 Cups flour
Mix butter and sugar till creamy. Add eggs, salt and vanilla beat until smooth. Blend in all dry ingredients, roll dough in ball, put in greased sheet slightly press with fork to flatten and bake in 350-degree oven for about 8 min.
Add about 1 cup of chocolate chips to this recipe for chocolate chip cookies.

Recipe: Created by Maria Klippenstein and baked often for her young children.

OATMEAL CRISPS COOKIES

1 Cup butter
1 Cup white sugar
1 Cup brown sugar
2 Eggs
1 Tsp. vanilla
1½ Cups flour
1 Tsp. baking soda
3 Cups rolled oats
Mix cookie dough as in order given,
roll into a small ball, press down and bake in a 350 oven
for 7 Min or until lightly brown.

OATMEAL AND DATE COOKIES

1 Cup butter
1 Cup brown sugar
½ Cup sour cream
¼ Cup milk
1 Tsp. salt
2 Cups rolled oats
2 Cups flour
Cream the butter and sugar. Add other ingredients in the given order. Mix well and roll to about ¼ inch. Cut with round cookie cutter. Bake in oven@ 350 for about 8 – 10 min until sides of cookie just start turning golden. Cool and spread date filling between two cookies.
Filling:
2 Cups chopped dates
½ Cup sugar (OPTIONAL)
3 Tbsp. butter
¾ Cup cold water
1 Tbsp. lemon zest or orange zest
Cook until thick and dates are tender.
Cool and spread between two cookies.
If desired use figs instead of dates

Recipe: This is a favourite cookie of John Klippenstein, his mother Helena Dueck Klippenstein, would bake a similar cookie at Christmas. This recipe is adapted from her recipe.

GINGER SNAPS

¾ Cup butter
1 Cup white sugar
1 Egg
¼ Cup dark molasses
2 Cups flour
1 ½ Tsp. soda
1 Tsp. cloves
1 Tsp. cinnamon
1 Tsp. ginger

Cream butter add sugar gradually, cream thoroughly. Add egg and molasses. Beat until smooth. Sift dry ingredients into creamed mixture and stir. Roll into a ball and dip in sugar, then press with fork.
Bake 8 – 10 minutes in 350 degrees.

Recipe: A family favourite

SYRUP COOKIES

2 Cups shortening (butter)
1 Cup syrup
2 Cups sugar
4 Tsp. baking soda
4 Tsp. vanilla
4 Eggs
Enough flour to make soft dough

Cream ingredients until light and fluffy add enough flour for soft dough to roll out. Cut with cookie cutter.
Bake in moderate oven until lightly baked. 8-10 min.

This is a Traditional Mennonite Heritage recipe

The Syrup pail also served as a lunch pail for Mennonite childeren in many of the conmunities.

CHOCOLATE COOKIES

1 Cup butter
1 ¼ White sugar
2 Eggs
1 ½ Tsp. rum flavour
2/3 Cup dark powder cocoa (dark Dutch or Italian cocoa)
Hot water or hot coffee to make paste
1 Tsp. baking soda
½ Cup Hershey chocolate chips
1 Tsp. baking powder
¼ Tsp. salt
1 ¾ - 2 Cups flour
With mixer in a large bowl mix butter, sugar, eggs and rum flavour.
Add to the bowl the chocolate chips, baking powder, salt and flour.
Place the powder cocoa in large cup with the baking soda. Then add and stir enough hot water or hot coffee to the cocoa to make a paste. Add to the dough mixture and mix all ingredients. If too dry add just enough heavy cream for softer dough. Roll into walnut size ball, press with fork. Bake at 350 oven for 8 – 10 min.

BIRD'S NEST COOKIES

½ Cups butter
¼ Cup sugar
1 Cup flour
2 Eggs yolks
1 Tbsp. milk
1 Tsp. baking powder
1 Tsp. salt
Mix in usual cookie method and roll out thin. Cut with small cookie cutter. Top off with a spoonful of meringue and a piece of candied cherries.
Bake in 350 ovens until light golden.
Meringue:
2 Egg whites (beaten stiff)
1 Cup fine sugar
2 Cups coconut (shredded)
1 Tsp. melted butter

Recipe used for holiday baking

SHORTBREAD COOKIES

1 Lb butter
2 ½ Cup flour
1 Cup icing sugar
1 Cup Rice flour or cornstarch
1 Tbsp. lemon zest
1 Tsp. flavour (vanilla, almond, lemon juice or crystallized ginger finely chopped)
Whip butter, icing sugar, zest and flavouring until smooth. Add flour and whip.
Roll out dough. Do not use to much flour for rolling.
Bake @ 350 till slightly golden

Recipe: Adapted by Maria Klippenstein

SOFT WHITE COOKIES (SCHMUANT KUCHE)

1 Cup butter
1 ½ Cup sugar
2 eggs
½ Tsp. salt
2 Tsp. vanilla
½ Tsp. baking soda
2 Tsp. baking powder
3 Cups flour
1 Cup thick sour cream

Mix butter and sugar together until creamy. Add eggs, salt and vanilla, beating well. Stir together all dry ingredients. Add alternately with sour cream, beating after each addition. Chill dough then roll and cut with round cookie cutter. Bake @350 for 7 – 8 min till lightly golden.
This goes well with the marzipan cream cheese filling and icing on the next page if you desire.

This is an old Traditional Mennonite Heritage cookie recipe Baked for family, and for the very young children as this cookie is very soft.

Marzipan Cream Cheese Filling:
In a food processor mix ¾ cup cream cheese and ½ cup marzipan until smooth and spreadable. When cookies are cool spread filling between 2 cookies then ice with following icing.
Icing:
Boil 1 cup sugar with 3 Tbsp. water until syrupy, beat 1 egg white with 1 Tsp. baking powder until stiff beaks form. Slowly pour hot syrup into beaten egg white, continue to beat until a smooth frosting forms. Ice cookie while frosting is warm.

The filling recipe was created by Maria it makes this cookie very delectable and delicious.

POP CORN BALLS

1 Cup clear Syrup
3 Cups Sugar
1 Lb Butter
1/2 – 1/4 Cup Cream
1/2 Tsp. Salt
1 - 2 Tsp. Vanilla
15 - 20 cups of popped popcorn
Tins of mixed nuts (optional)
In a medium pot melt butter and sugar until dissolved. Add the syrup and cream, bring to a slow boil, boil for 2-3 min. Take off the heat add vanilla and stir. Pour over the popcorn and stir to mix, Form and press into balls. Set on cookie sheet and let dry.
If poppy cock is desired just stir into the syrupy popcorn when warm a can or two of mixed nuts as desired. Do not form the balls. Stir and let dry on a cookie sheet. When totally dry transfer into large tins and seal with lid.

PEPPER COOKIES

1 Cup butter
2 Cups sugar
4 Eggs
1 Tbsp. vanilla
6 Cups flour
Pinch of salt
1 Tsp. ginger
1 ½ Tsp. black pepper
2 Cups cream
Cream butter and sugar add eggs one at a time and mix. Add flour, salt, ginger and pepper mix alternately with the cream to make soft dough. Divide dough in ½ and roll out to ¼ inch thick, cut with round cookie cutter. Place in greased cookie sheet and bake @ 350 till light golden.

This is a Traditional Mennonite Heritage Recipe
Recipe: This recipe was given to Maria from her Aunts Ann and Kathy Hiebert and was from her grandmother Maria Deorksen Hiebert.

RASBERRY NUT COOKIES

1 ½Cups butter
3 Cups flour
½ Tsp. salt
2 Cups almonds (blanched and slivered)
¾ - 1 Cups whipping cream
Sugar
3 Cups raspberry jam
Cream butter with the flour, salt and almonds, keep adding the cream a little at the time while mixing the flour mixture. Chill dough till firm. Sprinkle your working counter generously with sugar, place dough on sugar and roll to 1/8 inch thick. Do not use any flour for the rolling. Keep adding more sugar on counter if needed. Cut cookies with a small round cookie cutter, with a smaller round cutter cut a doughnut hole in the centre, to half of the cut cookies. Place cookies in greased baking sheet and bake @ 350 degrees for 7 – 10 min. Cool on rack then put jam on the whole cookie and place cookie with the centre hole on top as a sandwich. Put enough jam on the cookie so jam will squeeze up the centre hole.
Recipe: this is Maria's favourite cookie

HONEY PIROSHKY (BAGDAZKIA)

2 Lbs sugar
1 Lb honey
2 Cups boiling water
Pour boiling water on honey and sugar to dissolve
½ Tsp. gelatine dissolved in small amount of cold water and mix to hot honey mixture.
Combine following:
12 – 14 Cups of flour
2 Tsp. baking ammonia (heaping) dissolve in a little lukewarm water.
2 Tsp. baking soda (sift into flour)
½ Tsp. aniseed (ground) mix into flour
1 Tsp. mixed pfefferkuchen spices (mix into flour)
1 Cup Mazola oil
Mix all ingredients together and add and stir into the warm honey mixture.
Keep dough warm and covered. Roll out-use round cookie cutter-place tart jam in centre, fold over seal edge as for vereniki or perogi. Bake for 8 min in a 350-degree oven.
Icing: 1 cup sugar and 3 Tbsp. water – boil until syrup like. Beat 1 egg white and ½ Tsp. baking powder to form stiff peaks. Slowly pour syrup over beaten egg white, keep on beating until thick frosting stage. Keep warm while icing cookies.

This is a very old Traditional Mennonite Heritage recipe from Russia.

AMMONIA COOKIES

1/2 Cup butter
1 ½ Cup sugar
1 Egg
1 ¼ Cup cream
¾ Cup milk
½ Cup molasses
1½ Tbsp. baking ammonia
1 Tbsp. baking soda
1 Tsp. cloves
1 Tsp. cinnamon
1 Tbsp. vanilla
Flour enough to make soft dough.
Mix butter and sugar till creamy add egg and mix. Add the cream, milk, molasses, ammonia, soda, cloves, cinnamon and vanilla to butter mixture, but do not stir. Now add some flour and mix, keep adding flour a little at the time until you have a very soft dough that you can just handle. Let dough rest for 1 hour. Then roll out to ¼ inch thick. Cut with cookie cutters. Bake in oven @ 350 for about 8 min. When cool, ice with a thin icing.
Baking ammonia is available at ethnic Italian stores and other ethnic stores

This is a Traditional Mennonite Heritage Recipe. This recipe came from Maria's grandmother Maria Deorksen Hiebert, and originated from her mother from Russia.

HONEY PIROSHKY (BAGDAZKIA)

This is a very old Traditional Mennonite Heritage Recipe. These cookies are traditionally baked for Christmas.

This recipe originates from Russia and has a very unique flavour. They store well and can be baked a bit ahead of time before Christmas

AMMONIA COOKIES

This is a very old Russian cookie recipe. This recipe came from my grandmother, who would bake them every Christmas for the family

I continue to bake them for my family and are always a favourite. This recipe is a Traditional Mennonite Heritage recipe

BROWN SUGAR COOKIES

1 Cup butter
2 Cups brown sugar
2 Eggs
3 Cups flour
½ Tsp. salt
1 ½ Tsp. cream of tartar
1 Tsp. soda
1 Tsp. vanilla

Mix butter, sugar and eggs till smooth. Add flour, cream of tartar, soda and vanilla. Mix and roll out and cut with cookie cutter.
Dough is very soft so should be chilled before use.
Place cookies in greased baking sheet.
Bake @ 350 for about 8 min till slightly done.

Recipe: Created and baked by Maria's mom Mrs. Susan Neufeld. These cookies were one of her favourites and baked regularly

UNBAKED COOKIES

2 Cups white sugar
½ Cup cream or milk
½ Cup butter
4 Tbsp. dark cocoa (generous)
Pinch of salt
1 Tsp. vanilla

Put in pot and bring to rolling boil. Take off heat then add vanilla. Add the following while mix is still hot.
3 Cups rolled oats
1 Cup shredded coconut

Mix well with wooden spoon then drop with Tbsp. unto pan lined with parchment paper. Cool at room temperature and serve.

Recipe: Created by Maria and a family favourite cookie for a sweet treat or lunch box

OLD FASHIONED CREAM COOKIES

8 Eggs
6 Cups sugar white and brown
2 Cups milk
2 Cups whipping cream
2 Cups lard (or substitute with butter)
16 Tsp. baking powder
3 Tsp. baking soda
½ Tsp. salt
3 Tbsp. vanilla

Enough flour to make soft dough to roll out. Do not roll to thin.
Bake at 350 until very light brown bottoms, 7 to 10 minutes. Do not over bake and ice if desired.

This is a very old Traditional Mennonite Heritage recipe
Recipe by Maria's mom's family, the Hiebert's

NOTES:

CAKES & DAINTIES

WHITE CAKE

2/3 Cup butter
1 ½ Cup sugar
1 ½ Tsp. vanilla or rum flavor
3 Eggs
2 ½ Cups flour
3 Tsp. Baking powder
1 Tsp. soda
Pinch of salt
Milk

In a large bowl whip, the butter and sugar, vanilla and eggs, until smooth and fluffy. Add flour, baking powder, soda and salt. Add enough milk to make thin cake batter. Beat until smooth and light.
Pour batter into greased cake pan and bake @ 350 for 30 minutes or until done.
This cake is great for strawberry shortcake.

Recipe created by Maria Klippenstein

MARIA'S CHOCOLATE CAKE

¾ Cups butter
1 ½ Cups sugar
2 Eggs
1 ½ Tsp. vanilla
½ Tsp. salt
Mix and cream above ingredients then add:
2 Cups flour
3 Tsp. baking powder
Cocoa paste:
In small bowl mix the following with enough hot coffee or boiling water to make a paste.
½ - ¾ Cup of dark cocoa
1 Tsp. baking soda
Stir mixture until it forms into a smooth paste
Add cocoa paste to cake mixture and beat the batter until light and fluffy.
Cream or milk
Alternately add enough cream or whole milk to make a smooth medium thin cake batter.
Pour into greased cake pan bake 350 degree for 25 – 30 min.
Serve with hot caramel sauce. (recipe in this book)

Recipe created by Maria Klippenstein

RHUBARB CAKE

½ Cup butter
1 Cup sugar
½ Tsp. salt
1 Egg
3 Tsp. baking powder
2 Cups flour
3 Cups rhubarb (finely chopped)
Whip butter, sugar, salt and egg. Add flour, baking powder, flour and rhubarb mix with milk. Pour in to greased cake pan. Top with topping.
TOPPING:
1/3 Cup sugar
1/3 Cup chopped walnuts or shredded coconut
1 Tsp. cinnamon
Mix and sprinkle on top of cake batter.
Bake for 30 to 45 min in @350 degrees oven.

CHOCOLATE OATMEAL CAKE

1 Cup butter
8 Tbsp. cocoa (heaping)
1 Cup oatmeal: Mix together with 1 cup hot water. Let stand then add:
2 ½ Cups brown sugar
2 Eggs
1 Tsp. vanilla
1 Tsp. baking powder
1 Tsp. baking soda
1 Cup flour
Pinch of salt
Mix well and put 13 x 9 greased cake pan. Bake in oven at 350 for 35 – 40 min.

CHOCOLATE ZUCCHINI CAKE

½ Cup corn oil
½ Cup butter
5 Tbsp. cocoa
1 ½ Cup sugar
2 Eggs
1 Tsp. vanilla
½ Tsp. salt
1 Tsp. soda
1 Tsp. baking powder
2 ½ Cup flour
2 Cups grated zucchini
½ Cup sour cream or milk
Cream butter, oil, sugar, add eggs and vanilla, sour cream. Sift dry ingredients together. Add to mixture and fold in zucchini.
Pour into 9 x 13 greased pan. Sprinkle with ¼ cup of chocolate chips or leave off chips and ice to suit.

CARROT CAKE

1 Cup vegetable oil
2 Cups sugar
4 Eggs
1 Tsp. salt
2 Cups flour
2 Tsp. soda
2 Tsp. baking powder
2 Tsp. cinnamon
4 Cups grated carrots
½ Cup pecans
Cream sugar and oil, add eggs, salt and beat. Mix in flour, soda and cinnamon. Fold in the carrots and pecans. Bake in 325 oven for 40 – 50 min.
Ice with cream cheese icing (recipe in this book)

BROWNIES

¼ - ½ Cup cocoa
1 Cup boiling water
Mix together and cool.
¾ Cup butter
2 Cups sugar
2 Eggs
2 ½ Cups flour
1 Tsp. baking soda
½ Cup sour cream
1 Tsp. vanilla
1 Cup nuts
Cream together the butter, sugar and eggs. Add the rest of the ingredients including the cocoa mixture and blend together. Spread mixture on a cookie sheet lined with parchment paper. Bake at 350 for 15 – 20 minutes. Put icing on when still warm.
ICING:
½ Cup butter, ¼ cup cocoa and 6 Tbsp. milk, bring to boil, remove from stove. Add 2 cups of icing sugar, 1 Tsp. vanilla and ½ cups chopped nuts. Pour over on brownies while warm.

Recipe: Created by Maria's mom Mrs. Susan Neufeld

FRESH APPLE CAKE

4 Cups diced apples with peel
1 ¾ Cup sugar
½ Cup oil
1 Cup nuts (chopped)
2 Tsp. vanilla
2 Eggs
Mix together by hand the apples, sugar, oil, nuts, vanilla and eggs.
Then add:
2Tsp. baking powder
2Tsp. cinnamon
½ Tsp. salt
2 Cups flour
Mix everything together by hand and pour into a greased 9x13 pan.
Bake at 350 for 35 minutes.

MENNONITE SPICE CAKE

2/3 Cup butter
1 Cup sugar
2 Eggs
3 Tsp. baking powder
2 ½ cups flour
½ cup sour cream
1 Tsp. cinnamon
1 Tsp. allspice
1 Tsp. cloves
1 Tsp. nutmeg
½ Cup walnuts (chopped)
½ Cup raisins- add ¼ cup of water to raisins, heat in micro wave until hot. Then add 1 Tsp. baking soda to the hot raisins. Set aside to cool and add into cake batter.
In a large mixing bowl cream butter, sugar, vanilla and eggs together. Then add the flour, baking powder, all the spices and sour cream. Mix together with enough milk to make a smooth med. thin batter, now add the soaked raisins and nuts, mix. Pour into cake pan and bake in 350 oven until done and then ice with butter icing.
BUTTER ICING:
Put ¾ - ½ cup milk and 4 Tbsp. flour in sauce pan. Cook and stir until it forms a ball. Cool until only slightly warm.
Then add 1 cup butter, 1cup sugar, and 1 Tsp. vanilla. Whip until fluffy. Spread on cool cake.
Or use icing of choice.

GINGERBREAD CAKE

1/2 Cup butter
1 Cup brown sugar
½ Cup molasses
½ Tsp. salt
2 Eggs
Cream together, then add:
2 ½ Cups flour
2 Tsp. baking powder
1 Tsp. ginger
½ Tsp. nutmeg
½ Tsp. cinnamon
Mix together:
1 Cup boiling water
1 Tsp. baking soda
Cool to lukewarm
Add soda water to cake batter and mix and pour into loaf pan.
Bake in greased loaf pan at 325 degrees till done.
Great for Christmas served warm with Rum sauce. (recipe in this book)

Recipe: From Maria Klippenstein

OATMEAL CAKE

Pour 1 ¼ cups of boiling water over 1 cup rolled oats. Stir and let stand 20 min.
Cream ½ cup butter with 1 cup white sugar and 1 cup brown sugar. Add 2 beaten eggs, 1 Tsp. vanilla. Add rolled oat mixture. Blend well.
Sift together the following and add to the butter and oatmeal mixture:
1 ½Cups flour
1 Tsp. baking soda
½ Tsp. salt
2 Tsp. cinnamon
Mix well and pour into greased and floured pan bake at 350 for about 40 min.
In the meantime, prepare topping.
Topping:
¼ Cup butter
3 Tsp. cream
 ½ Cup brown sugar
¾ Cup coconut
1/3 Cup walnuts
Spread over hot cake, return to oven under broil until bubbly.
Be careful not to burn top.

APPLE CAKE

1 Cup oil
2 Large eggs
1 Tsp. vanilla
Beat together until light and fluffy.
4 Cups apples diced (finely)
½ Cup sugar
2 Cups flour
2 Tsp. baking soda
½ Tsp. salt
Mix the apples, sugar, flour, soda and salt, then add the oil and egg mixture and blend. Bake in moderate oven for 20 – 30 minutes. Cool and top with topping.
Topping:
1 ½ Cup icing sugar
1 Package cream cheese
1 Tsp. vanilla
3 Tsp. butter
Add icing sugar as needed about 1 ½ cups. Beat well together till smooth and spread on cake when cake is cooled.

Recipe: Created by Mrs. Susan Neufeld

MARIA'S CHRISTMAS CAKE

2 ½ Cups mixed diced candied fruit

1 ½-2 Cups whole green and red glazed candied cherries

2 ½ - 2 Cups raisins – dark and light

2 – 1 ½ Cups dried figs (cut in pieces)

2 Tsp. vanilla

1 ½ Cups of Maria's homemade marmalade

1 Cup Amerada liqueur

The night before you bake the fruit cake, combine the fruit, fruit preserves, vanilla and liqueur. Let stand at room temperature overnight.

Then add to fruit:

1 – 1 ½ Cups coarsely chopped Hazelnuts

1 – 1 ½ Cups coarsely chopped Pecans

Cream together until light and fluffy:

2 – 2 ½ Cups flour

1 – 1 ½Cups butter (use extra butter if needed)

1 Tsp. fresh ground nutmeg

1 Tsp. cloves

1 ½ Tsp. cinnamon

Beat together until thick and fluffy:

9 – 12 Eggs

1 – 1 ½ Cups brown sugar and ¼ molasses

Stir beaten egg mixture thoroughly into creamed butter-flour mixture.

Pour batter over fruits and nuts. Mix together gently but quickly.

Fill prepared 3 loaf pans. (3 Loaf pans lined with several layers of parchment paper)

Pat batter down firmly. Cover each pan with double layer of tin foil to seal the batter in the pans.

Place pans of batter into water bath (larger pan with water in bottom)

Bake in 300 degrees oven for about 2 hours.

Don't let water dry out, add more water if needed.

Remove tin foil bake for 10 – 15 minutes more if desired.

Remove from oven and cool.

When cakes are cooled (totally cool) remove from pans and remove parchment.

Wrap cake in gauze cloth soaked in Amerada liqueur. Seal and store each cake in zip lock bag in cupboard.

MARIA'S RUM BALLS

¾ Cups dark cocoa
1 ¼ Cups brown sugar
½ Cup butter
½ Cup cream
Boil until syrupy 4-5 minutes – cool for a few minutes
In large bowl mix dry ingredients:
3 ½ - 4 Cups graham wafer crumbs (fine)
2 Cups fine shredded coconut
1 ½ Cups almonds and pecans (mixed and chopped)
2 Tsp. rum flavour (Oetker Brand)
Mix slightly cooled cocoa syrup to dry ingredient mixture, blend, roll mixture into small balls, cool.
Melt semi sweet chocolate, add rum flavour and dip rum balls into chocolate, place on parchment paper till cool and chocolate is hard.
Store rum balls in an airtight container.

Recipe: Created by Maria, families favourite Christmas treat.

DATE SQUARES

1 Cup flour
½ Tsp. baking soda
½ Tsp. salt
1 Cup Butter
1 Cup brown sugar
2 Cups Rolled oats
Sift flour, baking soda, salt cut in butter, add sugar and rolled oats. Take ½ the crumble mix and spread in 9 x 11 baking pan pat down gently then spread the date filling on top and use the remaining rolled oat crumble and spread evenly on top of the dates. Bake at 325-degree oven for 30 – 40 min.
Date Filling:
½ Lbs Dates
1 Tbsp. Baking Soda
2 Tbsp. Butter
1 Tbsp. lemon juice
½ Cup water
Put all ingredients in a pot bring to a boil stir to smooth out the dates and mix. Cool to room temperature before using.

Recipe from Maria's mom Mrs. Susan Neufeld

NOTES:

PIES PASTRIES & DESSERTS

MENNONITE SHIJTA PIE

FRUIT CUSTARD PIE

PASTRY PIE DOUGH

5 Cups flour
1 Tsp. salt
1 Tbsp. baking powder
2 Cups lard
Blend lard with flour mixture, work together with fingers until crumbled, than prepare:
2 Eggs ¾ Cup cold water 1 Tbsp. vinegar
Blend eggs, water and vinegar together, pour into the flour mixture and work into a smooth dough texture. Do not over knead.

SAVORY PASTRY DOUGH

1 ¾ Cups, all-purpose flour
½ Tsp. Baking powder
Pinch of salt
7 Tbsp. butter, (chilled)
¼ Cup superfine sugar
1 Egg yolk
¼ Cup cream
To make pastry dough, sift flour, baking powder and salt into a large bowl. Cut the butter into small cubes and add to the bowl with the flour, then rub it in with your fingers until it resembles fine bread crumbs. Stir in the sugar.
Mix the egg yolk and cream together and pour into the pastry mixture. Mix together and then knead once or twice until you have soft dough. Refrigerate until needed.

FRESH STRAWBERRIE PIE

4 – 5 cups of fresh strawberries
1 9" baked pie shell
Pile all the fresh strawberries into the baked pie shell. Pour the cooled cooked glaze over the strawberries and chill. Serve with whipped cream
Glaze: 1 cup of crushed strawberries 1 cup of sugar 1 Tbsp. cornstarch in a small pot bring to boil the crushed strawberries, sugar and cornstarch. Boil until clear and a little syrupy. Cool the glaze than pour over the fresh strawberries in the baked pie shell.

MARIA'S PUMPKIN PIE

1 Small to Medium Pumpkin use a sugar pumpkin (for chunky pumpkin)

Wash and top open pumpkin and remove seeds. Place on pan and put in oven at low heat. Bake until inside pumpkin soft. Remove from oven and cool. Then scrape out all the pumpkin flesh. Place into large pot or bowl.

12 cups pumpkin

<u>Add to Pumpkin</u>

1 Can evaporated milk

8 Eggs beaten

1 ½ Cup Brown sugar

¾ - 1 Cup white sugar

1/3 Cup molasses

3 Tsp. pumpkin spice

1 Tsp. ground ginger

½ Tsp. fresh ground nutmeg

1 Tsp. cinnamon

¼ Cup melted butter

4-5 Tbsp. flour

Mix all ingredients with hand blender. Do not over blend, leave pumpkin chunky. Pour into unbaked pie shell, makes about 3 – 4 pies. Bake at 320 – 350 till done. About ¾ hours. For a smooth pumpkin pie peel and cut pumpkin and cook till done. Cool, then add above ingredients and blend till smooth. Bake as above.

Recipe: Created by Maria

MENNONITE SCHIJTA PIE (LAYER PIE)

Pie Filling

8 Cups whole milk

1 ½ Cups sugar

6 Tbsp. flour

5 Eggs (well beaten)

2 Tsp. pure vanilla

¼ Cup butter

Pinch of salt

In large pot add milk and heat. In bowl beat eggs then add the sugar, salt and flour, mix well. Add to the hot milk and bring to boil to thicken. Remove from heat, stir in the butter and vanilla. Cool filling until only slightly warm.

Pie Crust

5 Cups flour

1 Tbsp. salt

1 Tsp. baking powder

1 Lb. Lard or Butter

Blend ingredients until crumbled, then prepare.

2 Eggs

¾ Cup cold water

1 Tbsp. Vinegar

Put ingredients in small bowl, mix well then add egg mixture to flour mixture to make pliable dough. If needed add just a bit more water.

Divide dough into three parts. Roll out each piece to cover a cookie sheet. Do not roll out to thin. Bake in moderate oven until light golden. Remove from oven and cut in half, in the middle of the width of the pan. Cool.

To assemble pie: Use a flat serving tray large enough for the pastry sheet. Place 1 sheet of pastry on tray, then cover with some of the filling to cover, put another sheet of pastry on top of filling then again cover with the filling. Repeat until all the pastry sheets have been used and the last sheet is covered with all the filling. Sides can be trimmed if desired

Cover the whole layer pie (the sides and top) with shredded coconut.

Cool in the fridge for several hours before serving, best if cooled overnight.

This is a Traditional Mennonite Heritage Recipe
Originated from Maria's Step grandmother, Mrs Jacob Neufeld married to her father's father.

SLAB APPLE PIE OR RHUBARB PIE

Apple

7 – 6 Apples peeled and sliced

1 ¼ Cup Sugar

2 ½ Tbs Flour

1 Tsp. Cinnamon (optional)

Pie Dough: (enough pie dough when rolled out to cover a cookie sheet on the bottom and top)

Roll out half of the pie dough and cover the bottom of cookie sheet. Peel and slice apples into prepared pan cover evenly. Mix the sugar and flour in a bowl. Add the cinnamon to the sugar if desired. Spread evenly over the apples and cover with the top layer of pie dough. Crimp the edges to seal and poke top for air vent. Brush with some milk and sprinkle very lightly with some plain sugar.

Bake at 350 until done

Rhubarb

7 – 6 Cups (was up washed and 1" cut up rhubarb)

1 ½ Cup Sugar

2 ½ Tbsp. Flour

Using the same process as above to prepare your pie for baking.

MENNONITE RHUBARB, PEACH OR PEAR PIE

4 Egg yolks

1 Cup sugar

¼ Tsp. salt

Pie dough for one unbaked 9" pie shell

4 Cups Rhubarb, Peach or Pear

2 Tbsp. Butter (melted)

4 Tbsp. Flour

3/4 Cup cream

Cut the rhubarb into 1" small pieces to make 4 cups. Mix all above ingredients together with the rhubarb and pour into the unbaked pie shell. Bake in a 350 for 35 minutes or until done and custard is set.

OPTIONAL: In the meantime, beat the egg whites until firm add 1/3 cup of sugar and a pinch of crème of tartar. Beat until firm and peaks form. Top on the warm pie put under the broil for a few seconds until meringue is slightly brown. Cool and serve.

APPLE ROLLS

1 Cup Crisco
2 Cups flour
4 Tsp. baking powder
1 ½ Tsp. salt
1 Cup cream
4 – 5 Apples

Cut shortening into dry ingredients add cream and mix to make soft dough. Add more flour if needed. Put in fridge for 1 – 2 hours. Roll out and cut into squares. In each square put in ¼ of an apple (sliced), fold pastry over, seal and brush with milk wash. Bake in 350 – 400 degrees oven until golden brown. Glaze with icing while hot.

Glaze:
1 Cup icing sugar
1 Tsp. vanilla or almond extract
Mix with warm water to make spreadable glaze with a pastry brush.

Recipe: Created by Maria's mom Mrs Susan Neufeld

APPLE CRISP

4 – 5 Apples (peeled & slice)
6 Tbsp. butter pieces
1 Cup butter
1 Cup sugar
1 Cup flour
2/3 Cup rolled oats
1 Tsp. vanilla
1/3 Cup slivered almonds (optional)

In 9" x 13" pan add the butter pieces and top with the peeled and sliced apples.

To make the topping mix together by hand, the butter, sugar, flour, rolled oats, vanilla and almonds. Mix with fingers to make a crumble.

Spread over the sliced apples in the pan and bake in 350-degree oven until light brown.

For rhubarb and strawberry crisp mix the rhubarb and strawberries with 2/3 cups sugar and 1 ½ Tsp. corn starch, then pour into pan, top with the above recipe.

Serve warm with vanilla ice cream or whipping cream.

BROWN BETTY

This recipe is great to use up for not-so-fresh, bread.
In a glass buttered cake pan add broken bread piece until pan is filled.
Add ½ Cup of raisins and
1 ½ Cup chopped apples
Spread throughout over the bread.
In a bowl mix the following:
4 Eggs
2 ½ Cups light cream or a mixture of milk and cream.
2 Tbsp. melted butter
1 Tsp. cinnamon (optional)
1 Tbsp. cornstarch
Pour milk mixture over bread in pan. Bake in oven at 350 for 25 – 30 min.
Serve warm with whipped cream

Recipe created by Maria Klippenstein

MENNONITE RAISIN PIE

2 Cups Raisins
½ Cup Sugar
2 Tbsp. Cornstarch
¼ Tsp. Nutmeg
¼ Tsp. Allspice
¼ Tsp. Cinnamon
2 Cups of Water
2 Tbsp. Butter
1 Tsp. Vanilla
1 Tsp. Baking Soda
Pinch of Salt
Pie Dough for 9" pie pan (unbaked)

To prepare the raisin pie filling place raisins in a medium size pot, add the water and heat until boiling point. Add the baking soda to the hot raisins and stir, this plumps the raisins soft and juicy. Turn off the heat. In the meantime, mix all the rest of dry ingredients in a bowl. Pour and stir them into the raisins in the pot, mix well and turn on the heat and bring to boil. Turn off the heat and stir in the butter and vanilla. Pour filling into a prepared unbaked pie shell, cover with a top pie dough or make lace pie dough strips to cover.

Bake in 350 oven just to golden about 20 to 30 min. Cool to serve.

A Pie dough recipe is in this book

MENNONITE FRUIT PERISHKY

1 Cup Shortening (Crisco)
4 Tsp. baking powder
1 ½ Tsp. Salt
1 Cup cream or sour cream
2 Cups flour
2 – 3 Cups fruit, blueberries, cherries or finely chopped apple.

Cut shortening into dry ingredients add cream and mix to make a soft dough. Add more flour if needed. Put in fridge for 1 – 2 hours. Roll out and cut into squares or round. In each square or round place, a spoon full of fruit. Fold over the dough, seal and brush with a milk wash. Place in a prepared baking sheet, bake at 350 – 400 until golden brown. Glaze with icing while hot.

To prepare fruit: In a bowl place the fruit of your choice as mentioned, add to the fruit ½ to ¾ cup of sugar and 2 Tbsp. flour, mix up and use for the perishky.

Glaze: Optional

1 Cup icing sugar
1 Tsp. vanilla or almond extract

Mix with warm water or milk to make spreadable glaze with a pastry brush.

MENNONITE FRUIT PLAUTZ

1 ½ Cup Flour
2 Tsp. baking powder
½ Cup butter
2 Eggs (slightly beaten)
¼ Tsp. salt
1 Tsp. vanilla
1/3 Cup milk or cream

Add the flour, baking powder and salt into a mixing bowl. Then mix the butter into the flour mixture with your fingers to form a crumbly mixture. Blend the eggs, milk and vanilla then add to the flour mixture and knead to make, soft dough. Press the dough into a smaller cookie sheet, making sure that it is evenly spread.

<u>Fruit filling:</u>

Use any kind of sliced fruit such as plums, apples, apricots, peaches and cherries etc. Slice enough fruit to layer the dough pastry, into a bowl and sprinkle with about ½ cup sugar or to taste, if you have juicy fruit add 1-2 Tsp. of corn starch to the fruit. Spread evenly over the dough.

<u>Streusel Topping:</u>

1 Cup flour, 1 Cup sugar and ¾ Cup butter. Mix together the ingredients by hand to make a fine crumb texture. Sprinkle over the fruit. Bake at 350 until done and lightly brown. Do not over bake.

This recipe is a Traditional Mennonite Heritage recipe and baked in most Mennonite homes.

GERMAN MENNONITE FRUIT PLAUTZ

¾ Cup whole milk

4 Tbsp. Butter

½ Cup sugar

¼ Tsp. salt

In pot heat the milk, butter, sugar and salt. Set aside and cool to lukewarm.

¼ Cup warm water

1 Tbsp. yeast

1 ¼ Tsp. sugar

Add into the bowl in kitchen aid mixer the yeast, water and sugar. Let the yeast dissolve and soften. Then add to the yeast the lukewarm milk mixture.

1 Egg

3 – 4 Cups flour

Next add the 1 slightly beaten egg and gradually add the flour and mix to make soft, but not sticky dough. Place the dough in a large greased bowl, cover with plastic wrap. Put in a warm place and let rise till double in bulk.

When dough has risen, place dough on a floured surface and roll out to cover a cookie baking sheet. Let the dough sit in warm place while you prepare the fruit.

Any fruit can be used such as sliced prune plum, peaches, rhubarb, apples arranged on top of the dough in neat rows. Also, cherry pie filling or lemon pie fillings can be spread on to the dough. Then cover the fruit or filling with the streusel topping. Let rise for 15 Min.

Streusel Topping:

¾ Cup sugar

¾ Cup flour

½ Tsp. baking powder

1 Tsp. vanilla

3 Tbsp. butter

Mix in a bowl with hand and until combined and mixture becomes crumbly.

Bake in a moderate oven 350 for about 30 minutes.

This is a Traditional Mennonite Heritage Recipe

MENNONITE APPLE STRUDEL

4 Cups Apples peeled and thinly sliced
½ Cup Walnuts (ground)
1 Cup Raisins
1 Cup Bread fine bread crumbs
¾ Cup Brown Sugar
½ Cup Butter
1 Tsp. cinnamon
1 Tsp. Vanilla
1/3 Cup Rum
Melted butter to brush phyllo dough
1 Box of phyllo pastry

In a fry pan on heat add butter to melt then add the sliced apples and fry until the apples are slightly done. Then add the sugar, walnuts, raisins and breadcrumbs. Heat mixture and add the cinnamon, vanilla and rum and heat. If mixture to dry add some more butter. Remove from heat and slightly cool mixture. In the meantime, prepare 9 – 10 phyllo dough sheets on a parchment lined baking sheet, brush each sheet of dough with butter and lay on top of each other to make layers. Then spoon all the apple filling at the ¾ point to one side along the dough, fold over the smaller flap over the apple mixture and next fold over the larger flap tucking under the over lapping dough to seal the strudel. Brush with butter and bake in a 350-degree oven until golden brown.
Serve warm with whipped cream.

Created by Maria Klippenstein

BUTTER TARTS

1 ½ Cups brown sugar
2 Eggs
1/2 Cup butter (melted)
1/4 Cup heavy cream
1 Tsp. vanilla
Pinch of salt
2 Cups raisins
1 Cup nuts (pecans or walnuts)

Mix well butter, cream, sugar, eggs, salt and vanilla. Then add the raisins and nuts to mixture, mix and fill unbaked tart shell to ½ - ¾ full. Bake at 350 for about 20 – 25 min. until golden brown or done.

PASTRY RECIPE

1 ½ Cup shortening (Crisco)
3 Cups flour
6 Tsp. baking powder
2 Tsp. salt
1 ½ cup cream or sour cream

Cut shortening into dry ingredients until crumbly, add cream and mix to make a soft dough. Add a little more flour if needed. Put dough into fridge 1 – 2 hours before using. Roll out and fit into tart shells

ICINGS, SYRUPS, & MORE

ICING FOR "AUNT SALLY'S CUPCAKES"

2 Tbsp. flour
½ Cup milk
Cook until thick. Cool
½ Cup butter
½ Cup icing sugar
1 Tsp. vanilla
Cream butter gradually add sugar and vanilla. Beat until smooth and creamy. Then add cooled milk mixture 1 Tbsp. at a time keep on beating until icing light and fluffy.

MENNONITE ICING FOR COOKIES

1 Cup sugar
3 Tbsp. water
Boil sugar and water until syrupy
1 Egg white
½ Tsp. baking powder
Beat egg white and baking powder until stiff, pour the hot syrup over egg white beat until very thick. Ice the cookies while the icing is warm.
If desired the icing can be flavoured or color added.

This recipe was used on most of the Traditional Mennonite Heritage recipes for cookies.

CREAM CHEESE ICING

1 ½ Cup icing sugar
1 – 8oz Package cream cheese
1 Tsp. vanilla
3 Tsp. Butter
In the mixing bowl of your mixer, combine all the ingredients. Mix until smooth light and spreadable. Use on your favourite cakes.

BUTTER ICING

¾ Cup milk
4 Tbsp. flour
In a sauce pan stir and cook milk and flour until mixture forms a ball. Remove from heat and cool until only slightly warm.
1 Cup butter
1 Cup icing sugar
1 Tsp. vanilla
In a mixer beat butter, icing sugar and vanilla, adding the cooled milk mixture in small amount at a time. Keep beating until very light and fluffy Spread icing on cool cake.

MARZIPAN CREAM CHEESE FILLING

3/4 Cup cream cheese,1/2 Cup marzipan 1 Tsp. flavouring (optional)
In food processor cream together, the cream cheese and marzipan until smooth and spreadable. Add flavouring if desired such as vanilla, almond extract or any one desired. Spread in between cookies, cake or use as filling.

CHOCOLATE ICING FOR BROWNIES OR CAKE

1/2 Cup butter
1/4 Cup Cocoa
6 Tbsp. milk or cream
Put the above ingredients into a pot and bring to a boil for 3 – 4 min. Remove from stove. Add:
 2 cups of icing sugar
1 Tsp. vanilla
1/2 Cup nuts (optional)
Pour over warm brownies or warm cake

PANCAKE SYRUP

1 Cup Brown Sugar
2 Tbsp. water
5 Tbsp. butter
1 Tsp. maple flavouring

In a pot but the brown sugar and water, bring to boil and simmer for 4 min.
Take off the heat and add butter, stir to melt butter. Add flavouring stir to mix. Pour into container and use warm on pancakes.

Recipe created by Maria Klippenstein

CARAMEL SAUCE

1/8 Cup of butter
2 Cups brown sugar
2 Tbsp. flour (heaping)
Combine the above ingredients in a heavy saucepan and carefully brown on a medium heat until sugar turns a medium brown. Add 2 cups of boiling water or as much as is needed for the consistency desire.
Boil 2 or 3minutes-set aside briefly- add 1 Tsp. vanilla, stir well and serve over warm Christmas pudding or cake.
For rum sauce add rum flavouring.
A spoonful of whipped cream adds a nice finishing touch.

HOT CARAMEL SAUCE FOR CHOCOLATE CAKE

2 Cups brown sugar
¼ Cup butter
¼ Cup cream
Place above ingredients in a sauce pan and bring to a boil over medium heat. Boil for 1 or 2 minutes, remove from heat and place sauce pan in a bowl of ice or some cold water. With a hand-held mixer, whip the sauce until smooth and thickened. Serve warm over chocolate cake. Add rum flavour for a rum sauce.

Recipe created by Maria Klippenstein

CREME FRAICHE

3 Cups Whipping Cream
4 Tbsp. Buttermilk or lemon juice
Pour cream into a bowl and add the buttermilk or lemon juice. Stir well to mix then cover the bowl with saran wrap and place the bowl in to a bigger container with medium warm water. Let stand for overnight in a warm place covered. The cream should solidify to crème fresh and separate from the whey. Drain the whey from the cream. Do not mix the liquid whey into the cream. Store the crème fresh in a sealed container in the fridge.

SPREADABLE BUTTER

1 Cup grape seed oil
1 Cup butter
2 Tbsp. water
2 Tbsp. powdered milk
½ Tsp. salt
Whip until butter it thickens and store in the refrigerator.

MENNONITE HOMEMADE HALVA

1 ½ Cup sugar
1/2 Cup water
Juice of 1/2 lemon
1 Tsp. vanilla
1 ½ Cup sesame paste (tahini)
Boil sugar, water, lemon juice to softball syrup remove from heat and add 1 Tsp. vanilla and 1 ½ cup sesame paste. Blend well and pour into a glass pan. Press down and refrigerate 36 hours

HOMEMADE B.B.Q. SAUCE

½ Cup dark molasses
3 Tbsp. brown sugar
½ Cup vinegar
1 Medium onion
3 Garlic cloves
1 Tsp. salt
2 Tsp. soya sauce
2 Tbsp. dry mustard
2 Tsp. celery seed
1 Tsp. of nutmeg, cloves& allspice
1 – 13oz tomato paste
13 oz of water (or more)
1-2 Tsp. liquid hickory smoke
Blend all ingredients in food processor. Pour on ribs or chicken. If not using immediately, pour in sauce pan and bring to boil. Simmer for 7-10 minute. Pour into sterile jar and store in fridge.

Created by Maria Klippenstein

BATTER FOR FISH & SEAFOOD

1 -2 Cans of Club Soda or Beer
Rice Flour
1 Tsp. baking powder
Salt
Flour to drench fish
Oil for deep frying
Pour soda into bowl then mix in enough rice flour to make a thin batter. Add baking powder and salt. Beat egg and mix and combine to batter.
Drench the fish or seafood in regular flour, then dip into the batter, totally cover.
Drop into hot oil and deep fry until golden brown and crisp. Remove from oil and put on paper towel to absorb excess grease.
This recipe is also great for onion rings and calamari and tempura.

FLOUR & HERB COATING FOR FRIED FISH

1 Cup flour
¼ Cup Corn meal
1 ½ Tsp. garlic salt
1 Tbsp. Paprika (optional)
1 Tbsp. parsley
Salt and pepper to taste
Drench fish in flour mixture and fry on medium heat on both side until lightly brown on both sides
and pepper to taste
Drench fish in flour mixture and fry on medium heat on both side until lightly brown on both sides

MENNONITE HERBS & SPICES FROM THE GARDEN

Above: Parsely: (Petaa Selj} used in mostly soups and sauces

Above: Summer Savoury:(Pepa Grout) Garden Fresh or Dried
used in fresh vegetable soup and dried bean soups

Bay Leaves (Lau Bladda) Used in canning and soups

Pepper Kernels (Pepa Jerna) Used in canning and soups

Star Aniseed: used in baking and chicken soup

Caraway Seed: for baking and cooking

Dill: (Dehl) used for canning and soups

Sorrel:(Suurom) used for soup

Rhubarb: used for baking and jams

<u>SOUPS</u>

NOTES:

MENNONITE SAUERKRAUT SOUP

3 - 4Qt water
4 Pork hocks
1 ½ Lb Mennonite smoked sausage (cut into 4 in pieces)
6 Cups Sauerkraut (for the homemade sauerkraut see in this book)
1 Small head Cabbage (chopped or shredded)
2 Large onions (diced)
4 Potatoes medium size (peeled and cubed)
2 Qt canned tomatoes
2 Cans tomato soup
4 Bay leaves
3 Garlic cloves
1 Tsp. red pepper flakes
½ Cup dill
2 Tbsp. coarse kosher salt
In large pot add the water, then add all the ingredients as described, to the pot and bring to a full boil. Then turn down the heat and simmer for three hours. When soup is done remove some of the hocks and sausage for serving and serve the soup in a bowl, with a little cream added.
This soup is a Traditional Mennonite Heritage recipe which was made in all the Mennonite homes and was served a lot in the cold winter seasons. The sauerkraut was homemade from cabbage grown in the garden.
 This soup has healing qualities when feeling ill.

Recipe created and adapted by John, Maria's husband from his grandmother Louise Dueck.

DIKJE MILCHE (BUTTERMILK SOUP)

4 – 5 Cups buttermilk
1 ¼ Cup whipping cream
Salt and pepper to taste
4 Eggs (hard boiled and cooled)
½ Cup onion greens
In a large serving bowl combine the buttermilk and cream stir to mix well. Chop or slice in thin slices the cooled hard-boiled eggs add to the buttermilk soup. Salt and pepper to taste, stir and garnish with the chopped onion green. (You can add other vegetables such as sliced radishes, sliced cucumbers)
Place in refrigerator for 1 hour and serve cold in individual bowls. This is a great summer soup served on a hot day.
This is a Traditional Mennonite Heritage recipe for summer soup
This soup was served in most Mennonite homes.
This soup was usually made with unpasteurized milk left out on the table to thicken overnight during the hot summer and then cooled.
The buttermilk and cream is a great substitute.

Recipe was adapted by Maria's mom Mrs Susan Neufeld.

BEET BORSCHT

1 ½ Cups cut up left over roast & juice or
1 Cup lean hamburger and 3 or 4 Tbsp. oxo
 10 – 8 Cups water
2 Onions
2 Tbsp. salt or to taste
3 ½ Cups tomatoes fresh or canned
½ Tsp. pepper
2 Cups shredded beets
2 Cups carrots (shredded)
2 Cups sauerkraut or cabbage (shredded)
2 Cups celery (shredded)
2 or 3 Bay leaves
4- or 5-Star aniseed
½ Tsp. summer savoury
1/8 Tsp. dill
Add all ingredients into a large pot and simmer for 2 hours.
Add whipping cream after done and simmer for 15 min. (Or add spoon of sour cream in bowl when serving)

Recipe: From Maria's mom Mrs. Susan Neufeld, directly off her handwritten recipe card.

SUMMA BORSCHT

Put 3 - 4 Quarts of water in large pot add
3 – 4 cups cubed ham and ham bone (picnic Ham)
Optional: add combination of ham and Mennonite sausage
Bring to boil: Than add following.
10 – 12 Cups chopped fresh spinach or (1 large bag)
5 Bunche's onion greens (chopped)
1 Medium onion (chopped)
1 Cup fresh dill (chopped)
1 Cup rhubarb or to taste diced (fresh or frozen)
3 Medium potatoes peeled and diced
Salt to taste
Simmer the soup for 1- 1 ½ hours. For serving add 1/4 cup whipping cream to pot or a little into each individual bowl of soup. Serve with roll kuchen (recipe in this book).
 Option: use sorrel from garden instead of spinach and the rhubarb.
Option: for ham is Mennonite farmer sausage.
This a Traditional Mennonite Heritage Recipe
This soup was made in all Mennonite homes, usually first thing in spring when greens appeared in the garden.

This version of the recipe created by Maria Klippenstein

OLD FASHION MENNONITE BEAN SOUP

Sort and wash 4 ¼ cups of small white dried beans, if beans are larger you can use a little less bean.

Put beans in large bowl and cover with water

Let soak several hours or overnight. Add more water if needed.

In large pot put 4 – 5 quarts of water add:

1 ½ Cups of cubed ham and ham bone (ham bone optional) or a   smoked pork hock.

Strain liquid off the soaking beans and add to pot of soup.

Boil for ½ hour then add:

2 Medium onions (diced)

1 Large Carrot (diced)

4 Bay leaves

3 Tbsp. summer savoury (peppa krout grown in all Mennonite gardens)

12 Kernels black pepper

Salt and pepper to taste

Boil for 1 hour or until beans soft and well done. Add a little more water if needed. Serve hot with fresh bread. This is a great healthy meal.

This is a Traditional Mennonite Heritage Recipe.

MENNONITE GARDEN FRESH (BABY VEGETABLE SOUP)

You need a garden or a very good market gardener for this soup.

I plant my garden in accordance so I can make this soup and grow the summer savoury. Seed the summer savoury early in the season for fresh or you may use last year's dried.

Gather from garden the very early and tiny vegetables:

Carrots

Summer savoury (a must)

String beans green and yellow

Snow pea pods

Potatoes

Onions

Gather enough to make for a smaller soup pot wash and leave whole the carrot, beans and pea pods. Dice the new potatoes and onion. Dice all the vegetables if not very tiny.

Put all the vegetables in a pot with 2 or 3 sprigs of summer savoury add water just to cover vegetables and bring to boil. Boil until vegetables are done this won't take long about 15 – 20 min. Then add to the soup whole milk to cover and a bit more, add 2-3 Tbsp. butter and salt to taste. Heat up until butter melted and soup is hot, but do not boil. Serve with fresh bread and this will be the best spring soup you have ever had.

If small vegetables are not available fresh and a little larger will do.

This is a Traditional Mennonite Heritage soup.

As a child, I would help my mother painfully gather up the tiniest and earliest vegetables and rob the potato plant for its first potato to make this soup. The summer savoury is best fresh from the garden.

FRESH TOMATO SOUP

In a large pot fry in:
3 Tbsp. of oil till translucent
1 Onion (finely chopped)
2 Stalks of celery
3 Cloves of garlic (optional)
Then Add:
5 Cups tomatoes (fresh crushed or canned)
2 – 3 Quarts of water
3 Tbsp. chicken bouillon
6 – 10 Pepper kernels
2 Bay leaves
¼ Cup fresh chopped parsley
¼ Cup fresh chopped basil (optional)
Salt to taste
Boil until vegetables are totally soft.
Mix in a bowl with cream or milk:
2-3 Tbsp. flour
3 Tbsp. sugar
Mix until smooth and add to soup. Bring to boil for 5 min.
Then add:
1 Tbsp. butter (large)
For a creamy soup:
Remove bay leaves and pepper kernels. Then blend the soup with a hand-held blender until smooth and creamy. Serve with homemade noodles or serve with dumplings as follows.
4 Eggs
1 Tsp. salt
Flour to make batter – that will drop off a spoon.
Drop by the spoonful the batter into the simmering soup. Put cover on the pot and boil the soup covered until dumplings are done. 5 – 10 minutes.
Serve

Recipe: Adapted by Maria from her mom's recipe Mrs Susan Neufeld

MENNONITE KOMST BORSCHT (CABBAGE SOUP)

4 -5 Quarts Water
1 Whole Small Chicken
1 Head of cabbage (medium size)
2 Large Onions
1 Can Tomatoes
2 Cans Tomato Soup
3 Potatoes
2 Bay Leaves
Large Bunch of Fresh Young Dill (chopped)
10 Whole Pepper Kernels
Salt and Pepper to taste
In a large pot filled with the water, add the chicken and bring to a boil. Shred the cabbage and slice the onions add them to the pot with the chicken. Simmer for 30 minutes. Then add the tomato and the tomato soup, diced potatoes, bay leaves, dill and pepper kernels. Add salt to taste and simmer the soup. Slow simmer soup for about an hour or until done.
Serve with fresh bread, also a little cream can be added to the individual bowls.

KJLETA MOUS (SCHLEPA MOUS)

This is a Mennonite hot milk soup, usually prepared for the evening meal. The soup was served with fried potatoes and some cold meats.

To serve 4 persons:

4 ½ Cups Milk

4 Eggs

3 Cups Flour

Salt

To make the crumbles for the soup place the eggs in a bowl and add the flour and the salt to the eggs. Work with your hands the flour and eggs by mixing and rubbing to make a very dry crumbly noodle. Rub the flour mixture to the size of peas or a bean.

In the meantime, put the milk into a pot and start to heat. As the milk heats up slowly mix in the crumble noodles and stir. Bring the milk to a slow boil and keep stirring. Boil for several minutes until the crumble noodles are cooked.

Serve: This soup is very good for an evening meal and gives a very relaxing feeling after a hard day's work or play.

HOMEMADE CHICKEN NOODLE SOUP

Using a large pot 4 – 5-quart size, fill with water and bring to a boil.

Add:

 1 Whole chicken or parts

1 Large onion

6 Tbsp. fresh Italian parsley (chopped)

4 Tbsp. salt

3 Bay leaves

10 – 15 Peppercorns

2 Whole star aniseeds

Simmer the soup for 1 ½ - 2 hrs. When done add 2 Tbsp. butter.

Serve and pour very hot over homemade egg noodles. (Noodle recipe in this book)

This is a Traditional Mennonite Heritage Recipe

All Mennonite homes made this soup. Traditionally, this soup was made and used to bring over to new mothers or to someone not feeling well

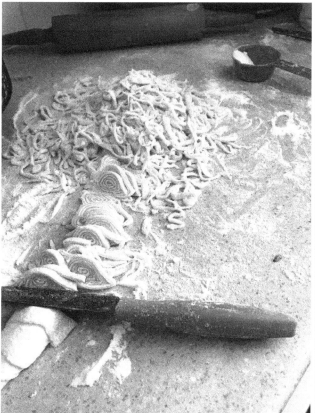

MENNONITE RINZ SUPP (BEEF BROTH SOUP)

1 Lb beef with bone or brown clear beef stock (freshly made)
Cut beef into small pieces then place the beef into a large pot and brown on all sides until very dark. This will give the soup a darker and better beef flavour.
Add 2-3 quarts of water and bring to boil.
Then add the following:
2 Onions cut in half
3 Bay leaves
10 Peppercorns (black)
½ Cup fresh Italian parsley chopped or
3 Tbsp. parsley flakes
Salt to taste
Simmer for 1 – ¾ hour
Sieve through a sieve to make a clear broth to serve.
Serve over homemade noodles. (Noodle recipe in this book)

This is a Traditional Mennonite Heritage Recipe

Recipe adapted by Maria Klippenstein

MENNONITE PLUMA MOUS

2 ½ Cups assorted dried fruit – prunes, raisins, apricots, apples
6 – 8 Cups of water
2/3 Cup of sugar or to taste
4 Tbsp. Flour (heaping)
½ Cup cream or more
1 Cinnamon stick (optional)
½ Tsp. ground cardamom (optional)
¼ Tsp. fresh ground nutmeg (optional)
In large pot add the water and the dried fruit and cinnamon stick, the fruit such as the apricots and apples can be cut into smaller pieces. Put on heat and bring to a boil, then turn down heat and slow simmer for 45 min. Fruit should be well covered with water.
Meanwhile mix together the flour, sugar, cardamom and nutmeg. Add the cream to flour mixture blend to make smooth thin paste. Add more cream if needed. Remove the cinnamon stick from the soup and add the flour mixture, stirring to prevent any lumps. Turn up the heat and bring to slight boil, remove from heat and cool.
Cool soup for several hours or overnight, it should be served cold. This soup is great with baked ham, chicken or potato salad or fried potatoes.
Other fruits can be used for this soup such as choke cherries or sour cherries.

This is a Traditional Mennonite Heritage Recipe
This soup was served in all Mennonite homes, usually for Easter or holiday celebrations. Although I add the spices for flavour, but these are optional, also the sugar can be adjusted to taste.
Recipe adapted from original Mennonite Heritage recipe, by Maria.

CREAM OF POTATO SOUP

3 Slices of bacon (optional)
1 Medium onion
2 Stalks celery
2 Cloves of garlic
4 – 5 Medium potatoes
4 Tbsp. chicken bouillon
2 Bay leaves
2 Tbsp. parsley
1 ½ Qt. of water or just enough to cover vegetables
1 Cup heavy cream (approx.)
1 Qt milk (approx.)
Salt and pepper to taste

Cook finely chopped bacon in medium sized pot. Add finely chopped onion, garlic and celery. Stir and cook for 5 minutes than add cubed potatoes, bouillon, bay leaves, parsley and water. Boil until all vegetables are soft and done. Take off heat. Remove the bay leaves and blend until smooth, add the cream and milk just enough to make a thicker cream soup. Add salt and pepper to taste and heat and serve.

Created by Maria Klippenstein

MEXICAN SPICY SOUP

1 ½ Pound Mennonite Farmer sausage
¾ Cup chopped onions
½ Cup chopped green pepper
2 Cloves minced garlic
4 Cups water
3 Cups tomatoes and juice
1 Large tin kidney bean (drained)
¾ Cup long grain rice
2 Tsp. paprika
2 Tsp. chilli powder
1 Tsp. salt and pepper

Cut sausage into bit size pieces, brown lightly in a large soup pot. Then add onion, peppers and garlic sauté until tender but not brown. Add water, tomatoes and juice and beans, rice, paprika, chilli powder, salt and pepper.
Simmer for 25 to 30 min, until rice is done and tender. Stir occasionally.
Serve with corn bread.

I served this soup to my children on their lunch break from school, on those cold winter prairie days

MENNONITE POT BARLEY PORRIDGE SOUP (JYOSHNE GJRET)

1 - 1 ½ Cups Pot Barley
1 Quart Buttermilk
Salt
Water

In a medium pot place the pot barley, add enough water to cover, bring to a boil and simmer until barley is cooked soft and water is gone. Add a little more water if needed to completely soft cook the barley. Then add enough buttermilk to just cover the cooked barley and heat to a boil, salt to taste and remove from heat. Cool to a cold temperature in the fridge or serve room temperature. Serve with some buttermilk to make the barley a little liquidly, (not too much). This should be served cold or room temperature.

This is a meal in itself, with a piece of fresh bread, and was served as an evening meal with a cut of cold meat usually in the winter months.

Brown rice can be substituted for the barley.

This is a Traditional Mennonite Heritage Recipe
This soup was a favourite in Maria's grandmothers house Mrs Maria Hiebert and is a favourite dish of Maria's

MUTTON LAMB BROTH

1 Mutton Lamb Shank or
5 – 6 Mutton lamb chops (cut into pieces)
1 – ¾ cup Pot barley
20 Pepper Kernels
2 Tbsp. Kosher salt
2 Bay Leaves
4 – 5 Quarts of water

In a large soup pot add water, mutton lamb and pot barley.

Bring to a boil add the bay leaf's, pepper and salt. Boil at a slow boil for approx. 2 hours. Then add to the soup the following.

4 potatoes peeled and cut into small cubes
2 Carrots peeled and cut into round slices
Add 1 small peeled whole parsnip

Slow cook for one more hour, then add 2 Tbsp. of butter.

Soup should be served with fresh homemade bread.

This recipe originated from Uncle Mr Abram Wiebe, he was a Russian Mennonite who was widowed with 4 small young children that he raised on his own. He also owned his own farm where he always had a flock of sheep, with other livestock for income to maintain his growing family. He also planted and tended a large garden, did all his own canning and baked most delicious breads,

SALADS & DRESSINGS

COLESLAW AND DRESSING

½ Cup salad oil
½ Cup mayo
¼ Cup sour cream
½ Cup sugar
½ Cup vinegar
1 Tsp. salt
½ Tsp. celery seeds
½ Tsp. pepper
Mix all the ingredients to make a smooth dressing.
Coleslaw
Finely shredded cabbage adds to the cabbage some shredded carrot, small amount of red bell pepper finely chopped and small amount of chopped onion or any combination you prefer.
Or use package of pre-shredded Cole slaw mix.

Recipe created by Maria

CAESAR SALAD AND DRESSING

DRESSING:
Place in food processor:
1 Egg
1 Garlic clove
2 Tbsp. vinegar or lemon juice
1 Tsp. dry mustard
1 Tsp. Worcestershire sauce
4 Drops Tabasco sauce
½ Tsp. salt or to taste
½ Cup freshly grated parmesan cheese
3 Fillet of anchovies (optional)
Blend all ingredients in processor, then with machine running trickle in enough salad oil to make a thick creamy dressing.
1 Large romaine lettuce:
Pour over coarsely chopped or pulled romaine lettuce. Toss and top with more coarsely shredded parmesan and bread croutons.

Recipe: Adapted by Maria Klippenstein

GREEN ONION SALAD DRESSING

2 Green onions (Stalks)
½ Cup vinegar
½ Cup oil
2 Tbsp. sugar
½ Cup Plain yogurt or sour cream
3 Tbsp. mayonnaise
½ Tsp. parsley
¼ Tsp. celery seeds (optional)
Salt and pepper to taste
In a blender add all the ingredients and blend until smooth and blended and thickened.
Use on your favourite salad greens and salad vegetables.

Created by Maria Klippenstein

BUTTERMILK AND BASIL DRESSING

4 -3 Tbsp. sour cream
4-3 Tbsp. mayonnaise
¾ Cup buttermilk
¼ Cup olive oil
¼ Cup vinegar
Large bunch of fresh basil
Salt and pepper to taste
Add all ingredients in a food processor, process until blended smooth.
Use on your favourite lettuce, tomatoes, cucumbers, onion, etc.
Recipe is great with summertime fresh salads.

Recipe created by Maria Klippenstein

BLUE CHEESE DRESSING

1 Clove of garlic (finely chopped)
3 Tbsp. sour cream
3 Tbsp. mayonnaise
1/3 Cup light oil
1/3 Cup white vinegar
1 Tsp. lemon juice
1 Tsp. salt
¼ Tsp. pepper
1/3 Cup blue cheese (crumbled)
In a food processor add garlic, sour cream, mayonnaise, oil, vinegar, lemon juice and salt and pepper. Process the dressing until smooth and blended and thickened. Pour the dressing into a bowl then add the crumbled blue cheese, stir to mix. Adjust salt and pepper as desired. Serve on your favourite greens or use as a veggie dip.
This dressing is great without the blue cheese if desired.

Created by Maria Klippenstein

PEAS AND APPLE SALAD

2 Cups canned baby peas (drained)
2 Apples (peeled and chopped)
Optional: add 1 apple and 1 cup another vegetable such as- finely diced cucumber, dill pickle, radishes, onion or onion greens. To this you can also add some diced cold ham or left-over cold meat and some diced cheddar cheese.
Dress with ½ cup or more with following dressing.

SOUR CREAM AND MAYONNAISE DRESSING

½ Cup sour cream
½ Cup mayonnaise
1 Tsp. lemon juice
1 Tsp. Dijon mustard
¼ Tsp. salt
A pinch of white pepper
½ - 1 Tsp. sugar (optional)
Blend all the ingredients together and serve over your favourite vegetable mixture.

COOKED BEET AND APPLE SALAD

2 Large red beets
1 Large apple (peeled)
1 large dill pickle
Cook the beets with skin on in lightly salted water for (35 – 60 min). When beets are cooked and cool, peel the beets and cube the beets into 1" pieces. Add the peeled apple and dill pickle chopped into 1" pieces.
Dress with ½ cup or more of horseradish dressing.

HORSERADISH DRESSING

1 Cup mayonnaise (regular or light)
2 Tbsp. fresh grated horseradish – or
4 – 5 Tbsp. prepared horseradish (non-creamed)
This dressing is very good and a zesty dressing for cold meats, fish and eggs.

FRESH GARDEN SALAD (PAPA SALAD)

1 Head of lettuce (crisp and cold)
½ of Cucumber (sliced and chopped)
1 Tomato (firm and chopped)
½ Cup onion (finely chopped)
1 Celery stalk (finely chopped)
½ of Red pepper or green pepper (chopped)
¼ Tsp. celery seeds (optional)
1 Tsp. salt
Pinch of pepper
¼ Cup of light oil
¼ Cup vinegar (or to taste)
Into a large salad bowl tear off bite size pieces of the lettuce, then add the prepared and chopped other vegetables. Mix Up. Sprinkle the celery seeds and the salt onto the lettuce and vegetables.
Important: to sprinkle salt on the lettuce and vegetables before the oil.
Now cover all the lettuce and vegetables with the oil. Mix up.
Sprinkle the vinegar over the whole salad and mix and taste. Adjust the vinegar if needed.
Important to follow the exact order that this salad is put together.

Recipe created by John Klippenstein and a family favourite

EGG SALAD

7 – 8 Boiled eggs (hard boiled) (cold and peeled)
½ to ¾ Cup finely chopped celery
1 Tbsp. chopped onion (optional)
1 ½ - 2 Tbsp. mayonnaise (enough as desired)
Salt and pepper
In a bowl finely chop the eggs, add the celery, mayonnaise, salt and pepper. Mix and serve in a sandwich. Makes filling for about 4 sandwiches.

MENNONITE FRESH GARDEN LETTUCE

Vinegar and Sugar
Cut from your garden-fresh lettuce. Clean and wash and dry.
Cut lettuce into bit size, put in a bowl and serve on the table.
Have on your table the vinegar and sugar. Place,
the amount of lettuce you want on your plate and pour some vinegar on lettuce and sprinkle with sugar and eat.

NOTES:

VEGETABLES

MENNONITE RED CABBAGE

1 Small head of Red cabbage
4-5 Slices of bacon
2 Apples
1 Large onion
3 Cloves of garlic
3 Cups of water
Finely chop all ingredients and place in a pot with the water. Bring to boil and simmer until cabbage very soft. – Add a little more water if needed for soft cabbage, but the water should be mostly boiled off when cabbage is ready to serve.
When cabbage is soft add following.
Mix and blend together:
½ Cup sugar
½ Cup vinegar
2 Tsp. salt
1 Tsp. pepper
4 Tbsp. flour
Add to the steamed cabbage in the pot bring up to a boil, taste test. Take off heat and serve.

Recipe: Created by Maria, is adapted from old German recipe

MENNONITE SCHMUA COMBST

1 Cabbage (small size or ½ head)
1 – 1 ½ Cups of raisins
2 Cups water
3 Tbsp. brown sugar
1 Tbsp. butter
1 ½ Tsp. of vinegar
Salt and pepper to taste
Finely shred cabbage and put in pot, add the raisins and water. Bring to boil and slow simmer until tender, about ½ to ¾ hours. (Keep adding water if needed.)
Then add the sugar, butter, vinegar and salt and pepper to taste. Bring to simmer for 10 – 20 min take off heat and serve. Serve with pork or chicken.

This is a Traditional Mennonite Heritage Recipe
This recipe adapted by Maria from her Mom, Mrs. Susan Neufeld.

CREAMED PEAS

Boil peas in pot until done/ then add
2 – 3 Tbsp. sour cream
1 – 2 Tbsp. flour
Salt and pepper to taste
Bring back to boil until thick remove from heat and Serve

CREAMED CABBAGE

Boil shredded or coarsely cut cabbage until done and soft.
Before serving Add:
½ Cup whipping cream (or sour cream)
1 Tbsp. butter
1 Tbsp. flour
¼ Tsp. caraway seed (optional)
Salt and pepper to taste
Bring to boil to thicken remove from heat and serve.

Recipe's created by Maria

STUFFED BAKED POTATOES

5 – 6Large potatoes
¾ Cup sour cream (approx.)
½ Cup bacon bits
½ Cup onion greens
1 ½ Cups shredded cheese
Salt and pepper to taste
Choose large baking potatoes, wash and bake in moderate oven until done.
Remove from oven and cool so you can handle the potato. Cut potato in half-length wise and scoop out both halves of the potato being careful not to break the baked peel.
Place all the potato in a large bowl, then add:
Sour cream, freshly made bacon bits, chopped onion, shredded cheese, salt and pepper. Mix and mash the potato and the ingredients until smooth. Fill the potato peel shells until heaping full. You will not use all the peel shells.
To serve heat potato in oven until heated through, garnish with extra cheese if desired.
These potatoes can be made ahead of time and heated when needed.

Recipe created by Maria Klippenstein

SCALLOPED POTATOES

5-6 large Potatoes
1 Onion (finely chopped)
2 ½ Cups Milk
½ Cup Heavy cream
8 slices of bacon (optional)
Salt and pepper to taste
Peel and cut potatoes in to thin slices and put into a pot with some water to par boil. Remove from heat drain off all the water and place par boil potatoes into a glass or ceramic baking dish. Add the finely chopped onions and pour the milk and cream over the potatoes. Salt and pepper to taste. Optional: Layer the bacon over the potatoes on top. Bake the potatoes in the oven at 350 for 45 min or until done.

OVEN-BAKED POTATO CRISPS

5-6 Potatoes
Parsley
Salt
Olive oil or butter

Wash and peel potatoes, slice each potato into ½ inch thick round slices and place each slice evenly into a large cookie pan until pan is covered, salt the top of potatoes and sprinkle with parsley.

Add ½ cup of oil or 6 Tbsp. of butter to pan, place into a hot 375-degree oven and bake until done and golden. Serve hot and can substitute for fries.

Recipe created by Maria Klippenstein

FRIED RAW POTATOES (Rehve Jehbrodne Erdjokke)

5 – 6 Potatoes washed and peeled and very thinly sliced.

Place a cast iron frying pan on stove with oil and heat till hot. Add the sliced potatoes to the pan and fry at high heat until potatoes brown, when bottom is brown turn potatoes and keep frying some more, then add a ¼ cup water to the pan of potatoes, salt and pepper to taste. Put a lid on the pan, turn down heat and steam until potatoes are totally done about 10 min.
Serve potatoes:
With condiment of raw sliced onion that have marinated in vinegar for 20 minutes.
To serve the onion on the plate, sprinkle some sugar on the onion and eat with the potato as a condiment.
This potato recipe was served in most Mennonite homes for the evening meals.
The onion condiment was served in Maria's home and is delicious with the potatoes.

This is a Traditional Mennonite Heritage Recipe.

MENNONITE POTATO SALAD

5 Cooked med potatoes (cold)
8 – 12 Eggs hard boiled (cold)
1 Celery stalk (finely chopped)
3 Tbsp. onion or onion greens (finely chopped)
½ Cup mayonnaise
½ Cup sour cream
½ Cup cream
1 Tbsp. prepared mustard
Salt and pepper to taste

In a large bowl add the chopped cold potatoes, eggs and onions.
Add all the other ingredients into a small bowl and mix well for a dressing.
Pour dressing over the egg and potato and mix well.
Add salt and pepper to taste. Keep refrigerated and serve cold.

Recipe Created by Maria Klippenstein

LATKES

3 – 4 Potatoes (medium size)
1 Onion
2 Eggs
2 Tbsp. Flour (optional)
Salt and pepper to taste
Grape seed oil for frying

Into a large bowl shred, the raw peeled potatoes, potatoes can also be pre-boiled.

Shred the potatoes the potatoes should be shredded long and stringy.

Add the finely chopped onion and the beaten eggs to the shredded potatoes.

Stir to mix. Salt and pepper to taste.

In a large skillet add oil to cover bottom to an inch depth. Heat oil then add the potato mixture by the spoon full into pan, keeping the potato together in a heap.

Fry until brown on one side turn over and repeat.

Serve with freshly made apple sauce and sour cream.

A little spoon of caviar on top is great.

STUFFED RED PEPPERS

5-6 Red peppers (Large)
4 Cups cooked rice
2 Onions (chopped)
1 ½ Lb. Ground pork
5 Cloves garlic
½ Cup chopped fresh Basil
Juice of 1 lemon
Salt and pepper to taste

To prepare the peppers cut the very top of peppers to make cavity and remove all seeds.

Next mix together the rice, onion, pork, garlic, basil and lemon juice. Season to taste and stuff the peppers, then place into the roaster. Add oil to the bottom of roaster and top the peppers with the following sauce.

Blend in food processor:

4 fresh tomatoes, 1 small can tomato paste, 3 Tbsp. parsley and 2 Tbsp. oregano, salt and pepper to taste.

Pour the tomato sauce over the peppers and bake in 350-degree oven for about 1 hr.

Recipe created by Maria Klippenstein

NOTES:

BEEF & SELECT MEAT

B.B.Q. BEEF TENDERLOIN

1 Whole beef tenderloin
Paste to cover beef:
1 ½ Cup Cornstarch
1 Cup olive oil or grape seed oil
3 Tbsp. coarse pepper
2 -3 Tsp. salt
¼ Cup dry mustard or Dijon mustard
3 Cloves Garlic (finely crushed and chopped)
2 Tsp. steak spice

Mix all the ingredients into a smooth paste, if more moisture is needed for the paste incorporate more oil. When mixture is a smooth paste cover the tenderloin of beef on all sides until totally covered. Let rest for 30 minutes.

Heat up B.Q. to moderate temperature and place beef on grill. Grill to desired doneness. The coating will charcoal darker on the outside, but the beef will be tender and good on the inside. The coating can be removed or sliced through with the meat when slicing the beef.

Recipe created by Maria Klippenstein

MENNONITE HOLOPJCHA (CABBAGE ROLLS)

2 Lbs hamburger
2 Cups rice (pare boiled or done)
1 Onion (large) chopped
1 -2 Green peppers (chopped)
1 Egg
Salt and pepper to taste
4 – 5 Tins of tomato soup
2 Head of cabbage (pare boiled)
1 Cup sauerkraut (strained) optional

Mix all ingredients and take a small hand full of the meat mixture and put into one end of softened cabbage leave and fold side edge over and roll till tightly rolled and meat sealed in the cabbage. Repeat until all the meat is gone. Before starting to prepare the roaster, put in 1 can of the tomato soup with 1 can of water. Place each cabbage roll into the roaster as being made. Optional spread some of the sauerkraut on top of the layers of cabbage rolls.

Mix the remaining cans of tomato soup with equal part of water. Pour over the cabbage rolls, cover with loose cabbage leaves and bake at 325 or 300 for about 2 hr.

(Soften the cabbage by pare boiling the cabbage covered in water.)

This is a Traditional Mennonite Heritage recipe served in all homes
Recipe: This variation was given to Maria by Mrs. Regier, from Winnipeg, the owner of the Regiers Grocery Store, on Higgens Ave.

PASTRY MEAT ROLL

Meat Filling:

1 ½ Lb hamburger

3 Slices bacon (finely chopped)

1 Onion (finely chopped)

1 Green pepper (finely chopped)

3 Tbsp. soy sauce

5 Tbsp. cream

Salt and pepper to taste

Mix all the ingredients, salt and pepper to taste, set aside while making pastry.

Pastry:

3 Cups flour

4 Tsp. baking powder

1 Tsp. salt

½ Cup butter (very hard or frozen)

Milk to make soft and moist dough

Mix all dry ingredients, and then work in the butter which has been cut into small chunks.
Do not over work; butter should stay chunky in the dough. Add enough milk to make soft moist dough. Flour the work area and roll out the dough into a rectangle shape.

Roll out fairly thin. Spread the meat mixture all over the rolled pastry, leaving 1-inch edge bare. Then roll the pastry and meat as you would roll for jelly roll, from the wide side of the dough. Seal the end by folding under.

Place the meat roll into large cookie baking sheet, in a crescent shape. Cut slash holes into top of roll and milk wash. Bake in 325 oven for ¾ to 1 hour. When done serve hot, sliced into 2-inch-thick slices. Serve with mushroom gravy.

Recipe created by Maria Klippenstein

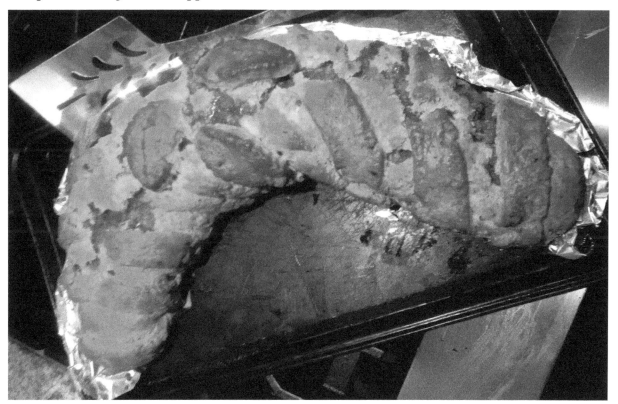

124

MENNONITE MEAT AND CABBAGE
(SAURKRAUT FILLED BUNS)

Dough for buns:

1 ½ cups of warm water

2 Tbsp. sugar

2 Tbsp. yeast   Dissolve the yeast in the warm water and sugar

Then add to yeast mixture

1 Egg (beaten)

¼ Cup soft butter

2 Tbsp. sugar

1 Tsp. salt

 Add enough flour to make a soft dough, knead until smooth, cover and let rise in warm place until double in bulk.

Meat Filling:

1 ¼ LB of Hamburger

5 – 6 Cups of shredded raw cabbage or you can use 2 cups of sauerkraut.

1 Onion finely chopped

Salt and pepper to taste

In a fry pan sauté the hamburger, cabbage and onions until done, add salt and pepper to taste. Set aside to cool. When dough has risen to bulk prepare baking pans. Then cut dough to form buns, place a large spoonful of the filling in the cut dough and form the dough around the filling to encase the filling inside the formed bun, set in pan to rise. When all the dough is formed into the meat buns cover and let rise in warm place let rise until double. Preheat oven to 350 bake until golden brown.

MENNONITE KLOPTZ (FRIED HAMBURGER)

2 Lb Ground Beef

1 Egg

1 Onion (medium)

3 Tsp. soy sauce

4 Tbsp. flour

Salt and pepper

5 Tbsp. Olive oil

Place ground beef in large bowl. Add finely chop onion to meat then add soy sauce, egg, salt, pepper mix together by hand adding the flour as you are mixing. When fully blended form into small handful round meatballs. Place in heated oil in frying pan. Fry meatballs until brown on both sides and done. Remove from pan and serve. If you desire, gravy can be made from the browned sediments in the fry pan.

KLOPTZ in Tomato Sauce

Follow the above recipe for the Kloptz, brown on both sides, then add 2 cans of tomato soup and 1 ½ can of water slow simmer covered for 20 minutes and serve. Great served with mashed potatoes.

KLOPTZ in Mushroom sauce

Add to the fried Kloptz in the pan 2 cups of sliced mushrooms and enough beef stock to barely cover, simmer and thicken with some flour, salt and pepper to taste. Simmer for 15 – 20 min until thickened and done and serve

Good with mashed potatoes and schmua comst, great comfort food.

Recipes created and adapted by Maria

BURGER PATTIES FOR HAMBURGERS

3 – 4 Lbs Lean ground beef
4 Tbsp. dark soy sauce
1 Tbsp. black pepper (fresh ground or coarse ground)
1 Tsp. Salt
1 Egg
4 Tbsp. flour

Mix all ingredients and form into medium size patties about 2 inches thick. Using a large fry pan or skillet heated with some oil until very hot place the patties. At high heat brown patties on one side turn to brown other side keeping the heat high fry for 4 minutes, then add all the sliced onion on top of the patties. Move the patties a little to mix in some of the onion to the bottom of pan. Put lid on the pan or cover patties and onions on the skillet, turn down heat to a slow simmer until the onions are done.

1 – 2 onions (large and sliced into rings)
Serve hot with buns and condiments, burger and onions.

Recipe created by Maria and made this way gives the best burger anywhere.

SALSBURY BEEF STEAK

2 Lbs sirloin beef roast
1 Large Spanish onion
1½ Cup flour for drenching
1 Tbsp. Salt
2 Tbsp. pepper
Water
Olive oil for frying

Slice the beef into 1-inch slices cut slices into about 5 in x 4 in piece. On a chopping board and using a meat tenderizer hammer pound all the slices of beef several times on both sides.

Set a large skillet on heat and add enough oil to well cover the bottom of the pan.

In medium size bowl add flour, salt and pepper drench each slice of beef in the flour to cover both sides. Place each slice of beef into hot skillet and fry until brown turn and fry both sides, when brown remove the browned slices and continue to brown all the pieces. Add more oil if needed, when all the beef has been browned return all the slices back into the skillet. Then add the onion on top of the beef that has been sliced in onion ring style.

Add enough water to almost cover the beef and onions, salt and pepper to taste and simmer for 30 – 40 minutes until thicken gravy.

Serve with mashed potatoes.

Recipe created by Maria's father Mr Gerhard Neufeld, which he used to make when mom was sick.

GERMAN ROULADE

2 – 3 Lb inside round beef roast
STUFFING:
4 Slices bacon (finely chopped)
2 Cups fine bread crumbs
1 Onion (finely chopped)
2 Stalks celery (finely chopped)
1 Cup drained sauerkraut
3 Tbsp. parsley
½ Cup melted butter
Salt and pepper to taste
½ Cup warm chicken stock
Mix all the stuffing ingredients in a bowl
Flour to drench roulade
3 Tbsp. paprika

Slice the beef into thin slices, make sure slices are unbroken. Hammer each slice with meat hammer to tenderize. Then on each slice of beef at one end place some of the stuffing. Roll beef slice around the stuffing, with skewer, secure the beef roll or tie with string. When all rolls are made, drench each roll in the flour and the paprika mixture. In large fry pan place enough oil to cover the bottom, heat oil until hot then place each roll into pan and brown on all side. Place each browned beef roll into a roaster, when all rolls are done deglaze the frying pan with water and some beef stock. Pour the deglazing liquid over the beef rolls and bake in moderate oven for 45 minutes. Serve hot.

Recipe Created by Maria Klippenstein

MENNONITE SHALVA FLEISCH (SHAVED BEEF)

2 – 3 Lb Sirloin beef roast (boneless and frozen)

1 Large onion

2 Carrots

Salt and pepper to taste

Place the frozen meat on a cutting board and using a large sharp knife shave off the meat in small shavings. Work fast to shave all the meat so it will not unthaw.

Place a large fry pan on high heat with 4 – 5 Tbsp. oil, heat oil to high temperature, then put all the shaved meat in at once.

Cook and stir all the meat until some of the rawness is gone. Add the chopped onion, and the peeled and thinly sliced carrots to the frying meat.

Salt and pepper to taste and place lid on pan. Reduce the heat and continue to simmer in the meat juices until tender (add some water or stock if to dry) for about 20 – 30 minutes.

This is a very delicious and easy way to serve beef and great with mashed potatoes.

Recipe created and made in Maria's home and by her mom Mrs. Susan Neufeld

SWEET AND SOUR MEATBALLS

4 Lb of lean ground beef

2 Medium Onions (finely chopped)

2 Tsp. paprika

1 Tsp. chilli powder

2 Tsp. Soy sauce

3 Eggs

2/3 Cup rolled oats or fine bread crumbs

Salt and pepper to taste

In a large bowl mix all ingredients together until well mixed. Meanwhile heat some olive oil in a large fry pan, form small meatballs and place in pan to fill and fry until browned on both sides. Fry all the meat in batches. Remove the meatballs from fry pan and place in a roaster. When all the meatballs are done deglaze fry pan with making the following sauce and pour over the meatballs. Bake in 350 oven for 30 – 40 minutes.

Sweet and Sour Sauce:

Deglaze pan with sauce as following:

3 Cups Water

2 Oranges the juice and pulp

1 Cup Vinegar

1 Tsp. Oregano

1 ¾ Cups Brown sugar

4 Tbsp. Corn starch

1 ½Tbsp. Dry Mustard

Mix all ingredients and pour into pan to deglaze and thicken sauce, pour on top of meat balls. Bake and serve with rice.

MEXICAN HOMEMADE CHILI

1 ½ lbs. Lean hamburger
1 Onion
4 Garlic cloves
1 Green pepper
2 Can red kidney beans
2 Cups homemade salsa (see recipe) or any favourite salsa
1 Can tomato paste
2 – 4 Cups canned tomatoes
1 Jalapeño peppers (optional)
1 Chipotle pepper (canned) or chipotle hot sauce
3 Tbsp. Mexican chilli powder
1 Tsp. cumin seed
3 Tsp. cumin powder
Salt and pepper to taste
In large pot heat and add 4 Tbsp. oil and then add hamburger, break up and fry until done and slightly browned. Chop onion and garlic and add to the meat stir and fry for about 5 min. Chop green pepper add to mixture then add the beans, salsa, tomato paste and canned tomatoes. Bring up to a simmer then add chipotle pepper, chilli powder and cumin. Add some water or more canned tomatoes to the chilli if too thick. Add salt and pepper to taste. Simmer for 30 – 50 min. For added heat, add the jalapeno pepper.

Recipe created by Maria Klippenstein, a family favourite

BEEF STEW AND DUMPLINGS

1 ½ Lbs Cubed stewing beef
1 Large onion (chopped)
2 Carrots (peeled and sliced)
1 Small turnip (peeled and cubed)
2 Medium potatoes (peeled and cubed)
2/3 Cup pot barley
Salt and pepper to taste
 1½cups flour (to drench the cubed beef).
In a large pot heat enough, oil to pre-fry the beef. Put the flour in a bowl add
 salt and pepper, drench the cubed meat in the flour and brown in the oil
until brown. Then add all the cubed vegetables and barley cover with water.
Simmer at low heat for 2 hours, stir stew now and then.
Dumplings:
1½ Cups flour
3 Tsp. baking powder
½ Tsp. salt
3 Tbsp. oil
Add enough milk to flour ingredients to make a very stiff batter. When the stew Is done, drop 1 Tbsp. at a time of the dumpling batter over the stew. Cover with the lid and simmer for 10 – 15 min. Do not open lid during this time.
Serve hot.
Recipe created by Maria Klippenstein

LIVER AND ONIONS

1 or 2 Packages of thinly sliced Beef liver
1 cup of flour
1 Tbsp. salt
1 Tbsp. black pepper.
1 Large onion
Mix flour, salt and pepper in a bowel. Take liver slices and drench with the prepared flour.
Slice onion in slices and set aside
Heat a frying pan with some oil, when hot, add the floured liver and fry on both sides until brown.
When both sides are done leave liver in the pan but add all the onions and fry for 3 min. Stir the liver and around, fry 3 more minutes put on the lid on the pan. Now ready to serve.

VENISON STEW

2 Lb of boneless Deer Meat
2 Onions (chopped)
1 Turnip (peeled and finely cubed)
3 Carrots (peeled and sliced)
½ Cup pot barley (optional)
Flour for drenching meat
Salt and pepper to taste
Cut meat into cubes about 2", remove all and any fat and tendons.
Drench all the meat in flour seasoned with salt and pepper.
Heat some oil in a large fry pan or pot, when oil is hot, start adding the meat. Brown meat until all meat is brown in the pan. Add enough water to totally cover the meat and stir the bottom of pan to deglaze.
Then add the prepared vegetables and the pot barley. Salt and pepper to taste
Bring up to a boil, reduce the heat and simmer for 40-45 min on stove. Stir the stew periodically, if needed add a little water or consume.
Serve with mashed potatoes.

Recipe created by Maria Klippenstein and a family favourite

LAMB ROAST

1 Leg of lamb
½ Cup olive oil
3 Tbsp. oregano
2 Tbsp. Greek spice mix
3 Garlic cloves (minced)
1 Lemon
Salt to taste
To marinate:
With some of the olive oil rub the whole leg of lamb with the oil then coat the lamb all round with the minced garlic and herbs. Place into a zip lock plastic bag and seal leave to marinate for 6 – 12 hours.
Baking:
Pre heat oven to 325 degrees
Pour some olive oil into the bottom of a baking pan, remove the lamb from the plastic bag and place the meat into the baking pan. Make sure all the herbs and the garlic are on the meat and squeeze some lemon over and place into the pre heated oven. Bake at 325 for 3 hours.

Recipe created by Catherine Klippenstein McGregor

PORK

SMOKED FARMER SAUSAGE DINNER

2 Lbs of Farmer Sausage
Oil to fry
Cut the sausage into 2 ½ to 3-inch lengths, place into heated fry pan with enough oil to fry. Heat the pan to medium heat and fry sausage to a medium brown then place lid on pan reduce heat to very low for 4 min or turn off heat. Do not over fry. Remove sausage from pan and place in a serving dish. Serve with mashed potatoes or varenikas or Perogies or Noodles.
Serve the potatoes or perogies with this Mennonite cream gravy (schmaunt faht)
1 cup cream (milk can be substituted)
¾ - ½ Cup of Sour Cream
1 ½ Tbsp. flour
Salt and Pepper
After removing the sausage from the fry pan deglaze the pan with the cream, add sour cream and continue to cook and stir at lower heat. Stir in the flour to slightly thicken, stir in salt and pepper to taste. Serve on the potatoes or perogies or noodles.
Serve with mustard pickles

This sausage dinner is a very popular serving in a Mennonite
Family and is very tasty.

MENNONITE PORK FARMER SAUSAGE PIE

2 Lbs Mennonite pork farmer sausages
1 Onion
½ Cup cream
Salt and pepper
1 - 9" Pie Pan
Peel sausage from the casing and place in a bowl and mix. Add onion, cream and salt and pepper to taste. Mix well.
Roll out pie dough for top and bottom crust for pastry. Place bottom crust in pie 9" pie pan, place sausage mixture in pan and even out. Place top pie crust over sausage mixture and seal edge. Cut air hole in top dough and milk wash top. Bake in 350 oven for 30 min or until golden brown. Recipe should make 2 med meat pies. Serve with a fresh mushroom sauce. Good warm or room temp.
Pastry dough:
5 Cups flour
1 Tbsp. salt
1 Tsp. baking powder
2 Cups of lard
Blend ingredients until crumbled, then prepare.
2 Eggs
¾ Cup cold water
1 Tbsp. vinegar
Mix eggs, water and vinegar then add to flour mixture to make pliable dough.

Recipe created by Maria Klippenstein

MENNONITE FARMER SAUSAGE BRUNCH

3 – 4 Cups whole milk
½ Cup heavy cream
8 Eggs
12 Slices of white bread
3 Cups shredded cheese
2 Cups Mennonite Sausage (skin removed and crumbled)
Butter for bread
Salt and pepper

Take the bread slices and remove crust and generously butter on one side. Place half of the bread buttered side down in a greased 9 x 13 glass baking dish. Save the rest of the bread for the second layer. Spread half of the cheese on top of the bread and spread all the sausage meat on top of the cheese. Next layer the rest of the bread buttered side up over the sausage. Mix up the eggs and add the milk, cream and salt and pepper to egg mixture. Pour all the milk and egg mixture over the layered bread and spread the rest of the cheese over the bread. Refrigerate overnight. Next morning bake in 350-degree oven for 35 to 40 minutes.

This is a great breakfast dish served on Christmas morning.

PORK AND BEANS

Sort and wash 2 – 3 Cups of dried white beans. Place in large bowl and cover with water and soak for several hours or overnight.
Then drain the soaking liquid and place in large pot cover with water and bring to boil, simmer until beans are almost tender. Drain the cooking liquid then add to the drained beans the following:

1 ½ Onions chopped
6 or 8 Slices of good smoked bacon (chopped)
2 Tbsp. dry mustard
½ Cup dark molasses
2 Tins of tomato soup mixed with the 3 tins of water
1-2 Tsp. salt
1 Tbsp. pepper
Add 10 drops of liquid Hickory Smoke (optional)
Place into an oven proof bean pot, put in oven and bake at 325 for 1 ½ hours
Add more water if needed during baking, do not let get to dry.

Recipe: Created by Maria Klippenstein

MARIA'S BARBEQUED PORK RIBS

Place 2 slabs of pork ribs in roaster, cover and bake in moderate 350 oven for 30 minutes. Take out of bake, drain some of the fat and cut ribs into 2 – 3 rib pieces. Add the BQ sauce and return to oven and slow bake in oven at 300 - 325 for another 40 – 60 min.

B.Q. SAUCE
½ Cup dark molasses
2 – 3 Tbsp. brown sugar
2/3 Cup vinegar
1 Onion (medium size)
3 Garlic cloves
3 Tbsp. dry mustard (heaping)
1 ½ Tsp. salt
2 Tsp. pepper
2 Tsp. celery seeds
1 Tsp. nutmeg – cloves (ground) or allspice
3 Tsp. soya sauce
2 tins (5.5 oz) tomato paste
2 Tsp. hickory liquid smoke
2/3 Cup water

Place all ingredients into a food processor and blend until smooth. Add the B.Q sauce to the ribs. This has to be baked with meat or cooked and sealed for storage.

MENNONITE ZILTFLEISCH (HEADCHEESE)

5 – 6 Pork hocks (whole)
Salt and pepper

Place all the whole pork hocks in a large pot fill the pot with water to cover the hocks. Bring water to a boil turn heat down to simmer and slow simmer the hocks for 2 hours, until meat separates from the bone stage.

Remove from heat cool until slightly warm, remove hocks from the liquid. Save the liquid and remove all the meat and skin from the bones.

With a meat grinder or food processor grind up all the cooked meat and skin. Mix the meat with salt and pepper to taste and add 4 cups of the cooking liquid to the ground meat. Mix well and spread out evenly into glass square pan or parchment lined cake pan.

Set into refrigerator for overnight to cool and set. To store cut the headcheese into serving pieces about 3 x 4 in pieces. Place in ziplock bags and freeze if desired.

To serve take the cut piece of headcheese and place in a small pot with a couple of Tbsp. water, heat and stir on stove until thoroughly heated. Place a couple of spoonsful on the plate and pour a tiny bit of vinegar on the meat and serve with fresh bread or toast.

This is a Traditional Mennonite Heritage recipe that was served at breakfast.

MENNONITE GREIVA (CRACKLES)

How to serve Mennonite Greiva.: usually these are served for breakfast

To serve put the unthawed greiva into a small pot and heat until heated and bubbly. Do not over heat. Remove from stove and drain the greiva through a fine sieve. Press on the greiva until all the fat is drained off. Return the greiva back into the pot and place back on the stove. Add approx. 2 tablespoon of water heat and serve.

Serve with a slice of fresh bread, using small pieces of bread to pick up the greiva to eat with.

Salt and pepper to taste

This is a Traditional Mennonite Heritage dish.

GROUND PORK CABBAGE ROLLS

1 Head of sour cabbage
2 Lbs ground pork
2 Cups cooked rice
1 Egg
1 Onion chopped
1 Clove of garlic (crushed)
1 Litre tomato juice
Salt and pepper to taste

Put ground pork in large bowl and add the cooked rice, egg, chopped onion and garlic, mix well and add salt and pepper.

Take the sour cabbage and rinse with cold water and separate the leaves. Then take each cabbage leaf and a small handful of meat mixture, place in the leaf and roll tightly to make the cabbage roll. Place each roll into a large pot until all the meat and cabbage are used and the cabbage rolls are all layered in the pot. Then add the tomato juice to the pot, enough juice until the cabbage rolls are totally covered. Place on top of stove and bring to a boil, then lower the heat and simmer very slowly for 1 ½ hours. Serve with a dollop of sour cream.

BAKED HAM WITH GLAZE

Place the ham in oven roaster and place in 350-degree oven. Roast ham for 20 – 30 min depending on the size of the ham. In the meantime, prepare the glaze.

Turn down oven to 325 degrees and start glazing ham. Bake the ham for about 1 ½ to 2 hours in oven.

Ham Glaze:
1 Cup orange juice
1Cup brown sugar
1 Orange chopped fine with peel on
2 Tbsp. summer savoury
1 Tsp. yellow mustard seeds
1 Tsp. basil
¼ Tsp. celery seed
1 Tbsp. parsley

Mix all ingredients in a bowl and baste over the ham by a small amount while ham is baking. Use up the glaze while baking the ham.

PORK WIENER SCHNITZEL

6 Pork tenderloin slices, 1 inch thick
1 Cup milk
1 Cup flour
1/2Cup med coarse cornmeal
1 Tbsp. oregano or parsley
2 Tbsp. paprika (optional)
2 Tbsp. salt
1 Tbsp. pepper
Enough oil to fry the schnitzel
With the flat end of a cleaver flatten the pork slices, they will become larger so if desired cut in half after flattening. Place the flattened pork into a large bowl and pour on the milk to soak for about 15 min. In the meantime, prepare the flour mixture and herbs and spices.
Place a large fry pan on stove, add oil and heat. Remove the pork from the milk, drench in the four mixture, place in the fry pan and lightly brown all the pork on both sides. Remove from heat. Now ready to serve although the schnitzel can all be placed back in the pan for a few minutes with no heat on.
Serve with Mennonite red cabbage or apple sauce.
Homemade noodles or kielke go well.

MENNONITE REPSCHPEI(SPARERIBS)

These are pork ribs that have been processed with the greiva and pork lard in a caldron. These ribs are added into the caldron and fully cooked' When done they are removed to a pan salted and cooled.
Traditionally they are eaten cold for breakfast the next day and or until they last.
These ribs are like no other ribs you have tasted and a specialty in a Mennonite home
The method and recipe and how it is made are in this book
This is a Traditional Mennonite Heritage food

POULTRY & EGG DISHES

ROAST TURKEY AND STUFFING

12 – 14 Cups of breadcrumbs or cubes
¾ - 1 ½ Cups onions (finely chopped)
¾ - 1 ½ Cups celery (finely chopped)
1 ½ - 2 Tsp. salt
1 ½ Cups potato (mashed)
¼ - ½ Tsp. pepper
1 ½ - 2 Tsp. crumbled sage
1 ½ Cups Mennonite Farmer sausage or bacon (finely chopped)
3 Tbsp. parsley
¾ - 1 ½ Cup melted butter
¾ - 1 ½ Cup water
1 Turkey

Place bread crumbs in a large bowl. Add onions, celery, salt, pepper, sage, potato, sausage, and parsley toss together lightly with 2 forks. Add the butter toss again. Add just enough water to moisten stuffing. Mix well and season to taste. Stuff the turkey and bake at 350 for 2 – 3 hours.

Pineapple rings were always served as a condiment with the turkey, Maria's dad's favourite Recipe: From Maria's mom Mrs Susan Neufeld. She developed this recipe when Maria's dad went to the Niverville community Christmas turkey shoot. You could win a turkey for shooting the bull's eye target in a contest between several people. He was a good shot so he would always come home with the turkey. Stuffed turkey was not a Mennonite Christmas tradition, but mom became quite famous in the Mennonite community for her great turkey dinners and dad for his deadeye dick shooting.

Roast Turkey and Stuffing (page 195)

HOMEMADE SHAKE & BAKE FOR CHICKEN

2 Cups fine bread crumbs
2 Cups crushed corn flakes (very fine)
1½ Cups flour
½- ¾ Cup melted butter
2 Tbsp. oregano
2 Tbsp. parsley
1 Tsp. garlic powder
1 ½ Tsp. paprika
2 Tsp. salt and pepper

Pre-soak the chicken parts in milk and 2 Tsp. salt.
Mix all ingredients together and using your fingers incorporate the melted butter into the dry ingredients and spices.
Place the mixed ingredients into a zip lock bag. Place 2 or 3 chicken parts in the bag and shake to coat.
Place the coated chicken parts on a greased cookie sheet. Repeat until all the chicken is used up.
Bake in oven at 350 - 375 for 15- 20 min turn chicken and continue to bake until chicken is done.
(A variety of herbs and spices can be used as desired)
This recipe is also good to use for baked fish

This recipe created by Maria Klippenstein

ROASTED CHICKEN

Roasted chicken was one of the main staples in a Mennonite farm home.

The Chicken was usually cut into parts and roasted in a Porcelain roaster and served accompanied with baked Bubbat. (see recipe in this book)

I roast my chicken in the antique porcelain roasters and believe that it still makes the best tasting roast chicken.

All chicken was raised on the family farm and butchered by the ladies of the house or by the children as needed.

1 or 2 Roasting range chickens

Cut chicken into parts and place into roaster. Add a little oil or 2 Tbsp. lard. Add salt and pepper to taste. Cover with lid and bake in moderate oven.

Serve with the baked bubbat [Recipe in this book), potatoes and gravy.

GERMAN CHICKEN SCHNITZEL

5 – 6 Chicken Breast, skinless

1 ½ cup Mushroom, sliced

1 cup flour

¼ cup Cornmeal (med)

1 Tsp. garlic powder

2 Tsp. oregano or parsley

1Tsp. salt

1Tsp. pepper

Butterfly cut each chicken breast, using the flat of meat cleaver slightly flatten chicken breast some more. If chicken piece is too large, cut in half.

In a bowl prepare the flour mixture with the herbs and spices.

Place a large fry pan on stove and heat with enough oil to fry the chicken breast. Drench each chicken piece and place in pan fry on both sides until light brown. When all the chicken is done keep in frying pan add all the mushrooms place lid on the pan heat for about 4 min then turn off heat. Now ready to serve.

QUICHE

9-10 Eggs
1 Cup broccoli pieces or zucchini sliced (cooked a bit to el dente)
¾ Cup finely chopped ham or Mennonite farmer sausage (crumbled)
½ Cup onion green (chopped)
½ Cup red bell pepper (chopped)
½ Cup milk or cream
2 Tbsp. flour
1 Cup shredded mozzarella cheese
Salt and pepper to taste
Beat eggs until well mixed add all the ingredients mix well and pour into an unbaked pie shell.
Can be decorated on top with some sliced vegetables or thinly sliced tomatoes or sprinkled with a little cheese.
 Bake the quiche in 350 degrees oven for 30 min or until done.
Options: Other vegetables can be used as substitute.

Recipe created by Maria Klippenstein

MEXICAN HUEVOS RANCHEROS EGGS

1 Red pepper chopped
½ Onion chopped
1 Tbsp. pimento (pickled) optional
2 Cups canned tomatoes
1 Fresh tomato chopped
½ Tsp. pepper flakes
1 Tsp. ground coriander
1 Tsp. ground cumin
2 Tsp. parsley flakes
1 Chipotle pepper (optional)
Place all prepare ingredients in a large skillet with some oil heat and bring to a simmer until done.
8 Eggs
When the sauce is fully cooked and simmering, crack eggs into the sauce.
Place a lid on the skillet and slowly simmer until the eggs are done.
Serve eggs on individual plates with some of the sauce.
This is a great breakfast dish.

Recipe Created by John Klippenstein

MENNONITE CHEESE FACTORY & FLOUR MILL

Pictured are Mennonite cheese factory in southern Manitoba. Here is where the Mennonite farmers delivered their farm milk and creams to be processed into cheese and other products for food for the families. Circa 1895 at that time there were about 52 such small factories in southern Manitoba amongst the Mennonites to process their dairy supply.

Pictured here is the early New Bothwell Cheese Factory and the Board of Directors for the cheese factory. Circa about 1936. Of the members of the Board of Directors front row left is my Uncle Mr.John Funk.

The New Bothwell cheese factory has now become a world renown cheese maker and is supplying all major outlet Costco, Safeway, Superstores and all major and small stores with their fine products.

New Bothwell cheese is a big part of the Mennonite community and is a must at all celebrations where food is served.

Pictured here are Mennonite Flour Mills circa 1877 and 1893 in southern Manitoba in the Steinbach area.
Above left is the replica mill at the Mennonite Heritage Museum in Steinbach, Manitoba.

These mills were used by the Mennonite farmers to mill the grain they harvested into flour to feed their families. These mills were very subject to fire and quite a few or most burned.

PASTA, PASTA SAUCES & NOODLES

PEROGIES (VARENIKI)

Dough:

2 ½ Cups flour

1 Tsp. baking powder

2 Tsp. olive oil

1 Egg

¾ Cup water (warm)

Mix all ingredients and work to make smooth dough. Let dough rest for 10 – 20 minutes covered. Roll dough on floured surface, roll to a medium thinness. Cut dough with 4-inch round cookie cutter. Place 1 Tbsp. filling in one half of dough pull over other half and seal. Make sure seal is tight.

Filling: <u>Potato</u>

3 Cups potatoes (mashed)

¾ Cup onions (finely chopped)

½ Tsp. salt

¼ Tsp. pepper

¼ Cup melted butter (Mix all ingredients and use)

Filling: <u>Cottage cheese</u>

3 Cups cottage cheese (dry curds)

1 Egg

½ Tsp. Salt

½ Tsp. pepper

(Mix all ingredients until smoother and form together)

Fill a large pot with water and bring to boil, when all the perogies are made gently and individually put the perogies into the boiling water. Gently stir once and bring to simmer until dough is done. Do not over boil. Turn off the heat and with slotted spoon remove the perogies and place in platter with some melted butter. Serve with the following cream gravy and condiments.

PEROGIES AND VARENIKI (IN MENNONITE TRADITION)

<u>Cream Sauce:</u>

In skillet pre-fry some Mennonite sausage or bacon until done, remove and set aside. Then deglaze the skillet with:

2 Tbsp. flour (do not brown)

Then add

2 ½ Cups of cream

4 Tbsp. sour cream

Salt and pepper

Wisk and bring to boil to thicken the cream serve hot as a sauce with the perogies.

 This same sauce can be made without the sausage or bacon, just use a pot to heat and thicken the above recipe.

<u>Condiments served with the perogies are a must:</u>

Thawed frozen strawberries with the juice, fried onions, sour cream and creamed cottage cheese.

This is a Traditional Mennonite Heritage recipe and served in all Mennonite homes.
Recipe: Created and adapted by Maria from traditional Mennonite recipe

MENNONITE KIELJKE
Homemade wide rustic noodle with onion cream gravy

5 Eggs
5 Tbsp. water
1 Tsp. salt
2 Tbsp. olive oil

Enough flour to make a firm and smooth dough. Let dough rest covered with a bowl for 30 minutes. Cover working area with some flour then roll out dough to about 1/8th thickness. Cut dough into 2-inch-wide strips in the length of the rolled dough.

Meanwhile fill large pot with water and bring to boil. Then with a scissor cut ¼ inch pieces off the strips of dough and add to the boiling water. Work quickly to evenly boil all the noodles. Boil for 7 – 10 minutes until done. Drain and rinse. Place the noodles in a platter and mix with some melted butter.

Serve with Sippel Schmaunt Faht and Mennonite Farmer Sausage

SIPPEL SCHMAUNT FAHT AND SAUSAGE

In large heavy skillet fry cut pieces of the sausage, cook until done remove from pan and set aside. Leave all drippings and sausage sediment in the pan. Finely chop 1 onion, add to the pan and sauté the onions until soft and done. Sauté onion at lower heat and do not brown. When onions are soft and done, add 2 – 3 cups cream mixed with 2 Tbsp. flour to the pan and the onions. Add salt and pepper to taste. Bring to simmer stirring the cream until thickened all the while. Serve hot as a sauce over the kieljke and serve sausage alongside.

These homemade noodles are a rustic delicious noodle and a favourite with most Mennonite families served with the Mennonite homemade sausage. This Mennonite sausage is also available at some super markets although not quite the same as the homemade.

This is a Traditional Mennonite Heritage recipe.

MENNONITE CHOP SUEY

1 ½ Lb hamburger
1 large onion (finely chopped)
2 Cups carrots (peeled and finely chopped)
4 Cups cabbage (finely shredded)
1 ½ - 2 Tins of tomato soup
Salt and pepper to taste
Homemade noodles or thin egg noodle (Italian style)

In large pot breakup hamburger into fine chunks and fry, stir until done, then add the onion, carrots and cabbage, salt and pepper, stir fry for 3 min. and then add small amount of water put lid on pot and simmer until vegetables are soft and done. Then add the tomato soup bring to simmer and add hot cooked noodles, stir and serve.

This recipe is great with homemade noodles and very tasty.

Recipe: Created by Mrs. Agnes Harder Maria's aunt.

HOMEMADE NOODLES OR PASTA

8 Eggs
3 Tbsp. olive oil
1 Tsp. salt
3 – 4 Cups flour to start, additional flour to make for stiff dough.

In a large bowl add 3 cups flour and make well in centre of the flour crack the eggs and add to the well with the oil and salt. Mix all the ingredients add flour if needed to make stiff smooth dough. Cover with bowl and let rest for ½ an hour. Then generously cover your working area with flour and roll out the dough to 1/8-inch thickness. Cut dough into 3 in. X 5 in. pieces. Meanwhile bring a large pot of water to boil. Using a hand crank noodle machine or kitchen aid continue to roll a small piece of dough thinner. Then cut the thin strips of dough on the thin noodle setting into the noodles. Add a little flour to the cut noodle and lightly toss noodles to keep them from sticking. When all the noodles are cut, take handful of the noodles and sprinkle them into boiling water repeat until they are all in the water. Keep stirring the noodles as they boil. Boil for 8 – 10 minutes. Drain and rinse

To make the noodles the old fashion way: Roll out the dough into rectangle on a very generously floured work area roll the dough until very thin. Then generously flour the top of the dough, there should be a 1/8 in layer of flour on the dough totally covered. Then from narrow part of dough proceed to roll the dough like you would roll a jelly roll. Roll very tight. Take a sharp knife and start from the end and cut very finely the dough into very thin noodles. Toss the noodles as you work in the flour to keep them from sticking. When all the noodles are made place small amount of the noodles in a sifter shake to remove the flour, then sprinkle into boiling water.
Repeat until all the noodles are in the boiling water. Boil for 8 – 10 minutes. Drain and rinse.

The art of noodle making in a Mennonite home was done with pride and achievement.

RAGOUT

2 Lbs hamburger or leftover roast beef finely chopped
1 Large onion
3 Tomatoes
4 Carrots
4 Stalks celery
2 ½ Cups canned tomatoes
3 Tbsp. Parsley
Salt and pepper to taste
2 Tbsp. flour to thicken sauce (optional)
In a large pan pre-fry in 4 Tbsp. olive oil the meat until done, then add the finely chopped onions, tomatoes, carrots and celery. Cook in slow simmer with lid on until done about 15 min., then add the canned tomatoes, parsley, salt and pepper. Simmer for 30 minutes than add the flour to thicken and simmer for 10 minutes.
Serve ragout on cooked egg noodles. (flat or thin noodles)

BAKED MACARONI AND CHEESE

Sauce:
2 Cloves garlic (OPTIONAL)
½ Onion (small)
3 Tbsp. flour
 2 Cups Milk
¾ Cup Cream
½ Cup Cream cheese
3 Tbsp. sour Cream
Salt and pepper to taste
Thinly sliced New Bothwell Cheddar Cheese to layer 9 x 12 baking pan
2 Cups Macaroni (uncooked)
Sauce: in a pot to hold all the liquid add 4 Tbsp. of olive oil add the finely chopped garlic and very finely chopped onion. Put pan on medium heat and sauté until translucent, do not brown. Add the flour to the pan with the garlic and the onions stir to mix then add all the rest of the ingredients except the cheese. Stirring the sauce, bring to a simmer boil at medium heat to thicken, turn heat off.
In a large pot of boiling water add the 2 cups of macaroni, cook until done. Drain well and pour into a glass about 9 x 12 baking dish. Pour sauce over the macaroni and layer the New Bothwell Cheddar Cheese slices on top. Bake in a 350 oven until cheese is melted about 20 to 30 min. serve hot

Recipe created by Maria Klippenstein

MACARONI AND CHEESE

1 ½ - 2 Cups Macaroni
Enough hot water to cook macaroni, cook the macaroni until done. Drain and return the pasta back into the pot.
Then add to the drained pasta in the pot the following:
3 Tbsp. butter (melt into pasta)
3 Tbsp. onion (very finely chopped onions)
2 -3 Tbsp. creamed cheese
1 ½ Cup shredded cheddar cheese
New Bothwell cheddar cheese
Salt and pepper to taste
Add some cream if needed to moisten.
Turn pot on to medium heat, stir in all the ingredients and stir until all cheese is melted and heated.

Recipe Created by Maria Klippenstein

MENNONITE GARDENS GATHERING, PANTRY, & PRESERVING FOOD

The original self portrait Painting by Maria Klippenstein.

In the Mennonite Traditional Community, the garden was an essential part of the Mennonite way of life. Most, if not all of the food they ate and served at their table came from the gardens they grew.

Potatoes, cabbages and root vegetables were stored for the winter time. All other produce that could be preserved was processed to last for the winter.

THE POTATO PICKERS...

Original oil on canvas by Maria Klippenstei

CANNING FREEZING & PRESERVING

CANNING METHODS AND INSTRUCTIONS

The following instructions are canning methods that never fail and jars will seal and have a long shelf life.

Wash all jars in hot water and rinse well or put through the dish washer.
When all the preparation has been done of the product to be canned, place the clean jars into the bake oven at a low temperature of about 150 degrees. Place the jars in a shallow pan with some water in the bottom or place them on a cookie sheet.
Do not over heat the jars as this might crack the jars when canning product is poured into the jar.

All canning product should be on a very slow simmer boil before and when filling into the hot jars. Remove each jar from the warm oven individually as you fill them. Fill the jars 2 inches from the top, wipe the rims of the jar with a clean cloth, place the sterile lids on the jar and tighten lids. Try and work fast at filling the jars as not to over boil or over cook your products.
The canning is completed this method is fool proof and works every time and your canned goods should last 1-2 years in your pantry.

You can use this method of canning for tomatoes, pickles, relishes, jams and salsas etc.
This canning method should not be used for cucumber dills. See the cucumber dill canning instructions in the dill recipe page.

I find this method of canning works far better than the canner hot water bath.

CANNING TOMATOES

Ripe tomatoes such as the Roma tomato or any smaller firm tomato will preserve well.
Tomatoes
1 Large Pot
Pickling salt
Quart jars sterilized washed with lids
Wash the tomatoes to prepare for canning, remove any defects and the stems. Place a smaller pot of boiling water on the stove and keep water boiling, use this to blanch the tomatoes to remove the skin of the tomato. Submerge the tomato in the boiling water a small amount at a time for a few seconds then transfer the tomato into ice cold water, now remove the skin of the tomato. (I use my sink for the ice water) Place the peeled tomatoes, leave them whole into the large pot. When all the tomatoes have been peeled and placed in the pot put on the stove. Start to bring the pot to a boil and add I Tsp. of pickling to about each quart of tomatoes. Slow simmer and keep stirring so as not to burn on. In the meantime, place all your sterile jars into your bake oven at 150 degrees to heat the jars.
When the tomatoes have come to full boil for 4 minutes, turn down to a very slow simmer, remove one hot jar at a time from oven, and fill jar with the hot tomatoes, wipe the rim of jar and put on the sterile lid and tighten. Repeat this method until all the tomatoes are in the jars.

CANNING FRUIT

Peaches, pears, apricots, plums and other fruits
Sugar
Fruit fresh
Water
Jars and lids
Wash and prepare the ripe fruit. Removing peels, stems any leaves etc. For canning fruit always use blemish free and ripe fruit.
Canning peaches: To prepare peaches for canning remove the peach peel by dipping the peaches into a pot of boiling water for 6 – 7 seconds then remove, transferring them into ice water, the peel will easily strip off.
Cut and slice the peaches into a large bowl as you prepare the fruit for the canning jars. Sprinkle a little fruit fresh over the prepared fruit as you proceed.
Syrup for Fruit: 5 cups water to 2 cups sugar
In a large pot calculate the amount of syrup you will need for the amount of peaches you have. Use the formula given above to make the syrup you will need. Bring sugar and water to a full boil for 4 min. then turn down to a very low simmer until all the jars are filled with the peaches and pour boiling syrup on the peaches. Wipe the rims and seal jars with the lids. Ready for processing in the water canner.
I prefer to can my fruit without the water canner. I prepare all my fruit and place it into the syrup on the stove. Than bring the fruit and the syrup to a low simmer. I than fill my hot jars from the oven with the fruit and syrup, wipe the rim and seal.

SALSA

12 Cloves of Garlic
7 – 10 Hot Green jalapeño peppers
 6 -7 Onions medium size
20 -30 Peppers assorted (reds – pimentos – banana peppers)
15 – 20 Cups of Tomatoes (skins removed)
Chop up chunky the garlic, onions, peppers and tomatoes and place in large pot.
Then add to the pot with vegetables:
3 Cups vinegar
3 Small tins of tomato paste
¼ Cup pickling salt
2 Tbsp. sugar
2 Tsp. paprika
2 Tsp. oregano
2 Tsp. cumin seed
½ Cup chopped fresh parsley or coriander
Bring to a boil and simmer for ¾ hour – 1 hour. Pour into sterilized and warm heated sealer jars. Close with sealer lids to seal.

Recipe created by Maria

DILL PICKLES

24 Cups water
5 Cups vinegar
1 1/3 Cups pickling salt
1 Tsp. Alum (or place into each jar, alum the size of a pea)
In large pot bring to a boil the water, vinegar, salt and alum. Boil for 7 minutes. Keep liquid at a simmer boil while pouring into the jars.
Place in each sterile jar some fresh dill with the seed head and 1 garlic clove
In sterile jars tightly fill full the jar with washed pickling cucumbers. Fill all jars first in this way then pour to 1 ½ inches from the top with boiling pickling liquid. Seal with sealer lids. Immediately put in the hot water bath.

<u>Dill canning instructions</u>
 Put a 4 inch depth pan filled with some water for a hot water bath into the stove. Heat the oven to 350 degrees. Place filled jars into the water in the oven at the 350 degrees for 7 – 9 minutes. When you see the slight change of color to the dills then remove jars from water bath from oven and cool.
DO NOT HEAT TOO LONG

Recipe used by Maria every year makes crisp and tasty dills.

MUSTARD PICKLES

12 Cups Cucumbers
4 Cups Cauliflower
4 Cups onions
¾ Cup Pickling salt
Wash and finely slice the cucumbers into a large stainless-steel bowl. Cut or break the cauliflower into small pieces and add into bowl. Then peel and slice onions and add to the bowl, add enough water to the cucumber mixture to cover, add the pickling salt, mix add let marinate for 12 hrs. Then strain off all the salt water, slightly rinse and remove all water.
In the meantime, in a large pot cook the mustard sauce, stir when cooking, when the sauce comes to a boil add the drained cucumber mixture and continue to heat and stir until mixture comes to a full boil for 5 minutes. Fill the boiling hot pickles into pint size hot sterile jars, wipe rims and seal with lids.
MUSTARD SAUCE
4 ½ Cups sugar
2/3 Cup flour
½ Tsp. paprika
3 Tsp. turmeric
3 ½ Cups vinegar
1 Cup water
2/3 Cup dry mustard

Recipe created by Maria and enjoyed by her family

BREAD AND BUTTER PICKLES

5 Quarts of Cucumbers (thinly sliced)

1 ½ Quarts of onions (thinly sliced)

2/3 Cups pickling salt

Water for the brine

In a large stainless-steel bowl add the thinly sliced cucumbers and onions cover with cold water and add the pickling salt. Mix and let stand overnight about 12 Hr. Then drain the cucumber mixture well from the brine, making sure the liquid is removed. Then place all the cucumber mixture into the boiling pickling liquid on the stove bring up to a boil again and keep at a simmer while filling sterile hot jars. Immediately place lids on and seal.

PICKLING SAUCE:

4 ½ Cups Vinegar

4 ½ Cups sugar

2 Tsp. Turmeric

3 Tbsp. mustard seeds

2 Tbsp. celery seeds

In a large pot to hold the cucumber mixture place and bring to a boil the pickling sauce. Simmer the liquid for 10 minutes then add the cucumber mixture and follow above directions.

HOTDOG RELISH

12 Cups sliced cucumbers

3 Cups sliced onion

3 Red peppers (chopped)

½ Cup pickling salt

Put the sliced cucumbers, sliced onions, peppers and salt into a stainless-steel bowl. Add enough fresh cold water to cover, stir to dissolve salt and let stand for 6 – 8 hours. Then strain all the salt water off and slightly rinse and remove all the water. Then place some of the onion, peppers and cucumber in the food processor with pulse setting process until ingredients are finely chopped to a relish consistency. Repeat until all ingredients have been chopped.

In a large pot cook the following sauce for the relish; Stir and bring to a boil.

3 ½ Cups vinegar

4 Cups sugar

2/3 Cup flour

2/3 Cup dry mustard

1 Cup water

3 Tsp. Turmeric

½ Tsp. paprika

1 Tsp. celery seeds

Then add all the finely chopped cucumber mixture and bring to a boil for 5 minutes. Pour into sterile hot jars and seal.

Recipe created by Maria Klippenstein

ANTIPASTA

1 ½ Cups sliced and chopped onions (soak sliced onions in vinegar for 2 hours) drain before using
8 Cloves garlic (crushed and chopped)
5 Carrots (coarsely shredded)
6 Stalks celery (coarsely shredded)
3 Green peppers (chopped by hand)
4 Red peppers (chopped by hand)
1 Head cauliflower (coarsely chopped)
1 Medium jar sliced hot peppers
In a large pot add all the first seven ingredients and 1 ½ cup water, bring to a boil and steam the vegetables for 3 minutes. Turn off heat.
Then add the following to the pot with the vegetables:
4 Tins black olives (pitted) drained
4 Tins green beans (French style) drained
4 Tins sliced mushrooms (drained)
3-4 Tsp. Cayenne pepper
2 ½ litre ketchup (Heinz)
Juice of 2-3 lemons and ½ Cup vinegar
¾ Cup oil – ½ cup sunflower oil and ¼ cup extra virgin olive oil
4 Tbsp. parsley   Salt and pepper to taste (pickling salt)
Bring to a boil and simmer for 10 minutes. Pour into sterile jars and seal.

MEXICAN HABANARO SAUCE

2 Heads of Garlic (peeled)
5 Hot green chilli peppers (seeds removed)
15 Habanero peppers (very hot)
10 Peaches (ripe)
2 Papayas (peeled and sliced)
1 Mango (peeled and sliced)
2 Mexican chilli peppers
Place all ingredients in food processor and puree.
In a large pot bring to a boil:
2 Cups vinegar
3 ½ Cups of sugar
1 Tsp. pickling salt
2-3 Tbsp. of cornstarch to thicken
Stir and bring the sauce to a boil and thicken then add all the pureed ingredients. Stir and simmer until it comes to a boil and pour into hot sterile jars put the lids on immediately to seal. Very spicy and tastes great on burgers etc.

Recipe created by Maria and daughter Amanda

MENNONITE OLD FASHION KOSHER DILLS

1 ½ gallon jug of distilled water (store bought)
 20 - 25 cucumbers (medium size)
8 cloves of garlic
2-3 large stalks of dill
1 – 2 Peppers (optional)
1 small piece of horseradish (optional)
2 – 3 grape leaves (optional)
10 – 12 cups of brine
Brine:
 Use 12 Cups of distilled water and ¾ cup of kosher salt for the 2-gallon container. Take 5 cups of this water heat on stove add the salt to dissolve the salt. When all the salt is dissolved mix back into the other water and cool until water is cold.

Prepare the 2-gallon glass jar or crock container by thoroughly washing in hot soupy water. Prepare cucumbers washing in cold water. Layer the dill, garlic, leaves, peppers, horseradish and cucumber until jar is filled to 2" from the top. Packing it down a bit, now pour the cold brine into the crock until the cucumbers are totally submerged and under the brine. It is important that the cucumbers remain submerged completely under water during this whole process. To keep them under the liquid place a glass plate with some weight on top.

Keep them at room temperature for several weeks until the fermenting bubbles have stopped. Some juices might over flow during this process. Taste to test in between to get the right tang. Always make sure hands totally clean. Store in fridge when process completed.

CANNING FRUITS, VEGETABLES AND JAMS

Preserving and freezing all the great produce that is available during the summer growing season is such a delicious, healthy and economical part of feeding your families.

Canning the fruits such as peaches, pears and plums are tasty and healthy. No preservatives need to be added plus the best of fruits can be used. These healthy fruit preserves can be enjoyed any time, when certain fruits are not season.

Freeze fresh berries from the gardens that can be used to make fresh jams and sauces. Berries such as strawberries, raspberries, blueberries or any fresh berry of choice will cook up into delicious and healthy jar of jam or syrup.

Pickeling, canning and freezing the fresh garden organic vegetables is an economic and healthy way to feed your family.

If you can grow your own garden this is ideal, it is an enjoyable way to feed your family and everyone can be part of helping to produce your family's food.

In most areas there are excellent farmers markets or garden stands that sell fresh garden produce locally grown that are fresh and delicious.

In a Traditional Mennonite home food was canned, preserved and stored in fall to last for the whole winter and until the spring gardens again would produce.

Many more canning recipes are available then that are featured in this book.

This is a great healthy and organic way of food to serve your family.

MAKING SAUERKRAUT

10 to 12 Heads of cabbage (fresh from garden)
Coarse pickling salt
5 or 10 gallon Crock
Wash the crock with hot water to sterile. Then start to shred the cabbage and place the shredded cabbage in the crock. Shred about one cabbage at a time. As you place the cabbage in the crock sprinkle a small hand full of the pickling salt evenly on the cabbage. Then proceed to stump the cabbage in the crock until the juice forms. Then add another layer of shredded cabbage and repeat the salt and the stomp until juice rises to the top of cabbage. Repeat this process until all the cabbage is used. Juices should be to the top of the cabbage. Then place loose cabbage leaves over the shredded cabbage to cover. Place a large sterile glass plate over the cabbage and place a weight on the plate to weigh down, (I, use a well washed smooth heavy stone). Cover with a lid. Let this stand in a dark place at room temperature for about 6 weeks. Check once in awhile and remove the scum if it has formed. After the six weeks remove the loose leaves of cabbage and bag the sauerkraut and some of the juice, into small zip lock plastic bags and freeze.

Making sauerkraut was a Traditional Mennonite Heritage procedure
This process is done every year or so by John and Maria Klippenstein to make delicious sauerkraut and used in their recipes

Maria Klippenstein Making Sauerkraut

ICE CREAM BUCKET BREAD & BUTTER PICKLES

12 Large Cucumbers
2 medium sliced onions
4 Cups white sugar
1 Tbsp. Pickling salt
1 Tsp. celery seeds
1 Tsp. mustard seed
1 Tsp. Turmeric
2 Cups vinegar

Boil all ingredients except the cucumbers and onions.

Slice cucumbers into an ice cream pail pour the hot brine over them. Shake well... Now add 2 medium finely sliced onions.

Stir 3 times a day for 3 days while keeping the pail in the fridge.

The pickles last forever in the fridge and are very crisp and crunchy.

An Italian lady, who sold her garden products from her garden, gave this recipe to Maria. They are easy to make and very good.

PICKLED BEETS

16 Cups beets (cooked and prepared)

To prepare the beets: Boil washed, and unpeeled beets covered in water until they are tender. Remove the beets from the water and set out to cool. When cooled peel the beets and cut into about 2-inch pieces.

Brine:
3 Cups vinegar
3 Cups sugar
3 Cups water
2 Tbsp. pickling spice

Place vinegar, sugar, water and spices into a large pot and bring to a boil and boil for 7 minutes. Then add to the pot with the brine the cooked and cut beets.

Bring back to a full boil, then fill the beets and brine into sterile hot jars, making sure the beets are covered with the hot brine. Wipe the rim of the jars and seal tight.

Photo above of a more recent summer kitchen on my property

SUMMER KITCHENS, OUTDOOR BAKE OVEN & SMOKE HOUSE

A Mennonite Summer Kitchen is a small building next to the main house used for summertime cooking and canning.

During the winter they were used to keep your meats, sausage and baked goods.

Pictured here the vintage farm summer kitchens from a grandmother.

Hanging Mennonite Sausage into the smokehouse ready for smoking

NOTES:

MENNONITE SPECIALTIES,
SAUSAGE MAKING, MEAT SMOKING & CURING

MENNONITE FARMER SAUSAGE

40 Lbs. Ground Pork (fine grind)

Use whole front shoulders and portion should be 12 – 15 % fat to lean meat.

Deboned and all skin removed.

2 Lb No: 40 Hog Casing

Spread all the ground meat out on a table or counter, spread out to a 3" layer.

Then season the top of the meat layer with:

4 Tbsp. Black Pepper

3 Tbsp. White Pepper

½ Cup Coarse Pickling Salt

Thoroughly knead all the spices into the top of the ground meat.

Then turn over the 3" layer of ground meat again pat to a 3" layer.

Repeat with:

4 Tbsp. Black pepper

3 Tbsp. White Pepper

½ Cup Coarse Pickling Salt

Knead meat again thoroughly.

Then pour 2 cups of cold water on the meat (a little at a time) and knead the water into the meat.

Then let the spiced meat rest for about 1 Hour.

You will need: No: 40 Natural Casings

Soak the casings in lukewarm water in a large bowl. Rinse and unravel them as you need and use them.

After letting the spiced meat rest an hour begins to stuff the mixture into sausages with a meat stuffer. We make our sausage into about 28 inches in length. At this length they can perfectly hang over the rails in the smoke house.

Hang all sausages in smoke house leaving 1" – 1 ½ "gap between each sausage.

You will need:

1-2 Bag of Hickory wood smoking chips

1-2 Bag of apple wood smoking chips

Start the smoking fire in smokehouse making sure not to get a flame, but only smoking embers. Top the embers with some moistened smoking chips. Smoke the sausage for about 2-3 hours with continues smoke, keep on adding moist chips to keep smoke going.

Let the sausage hang in the smoke house overnight. Remove the sausage from the smoke house, bag and freeze the sausage.

This is a Traditional Mennonite Heritage recipe

Recipe adapted and created by John and Maria Klippenstein from their Mennonite family heritage and made every year.

NOTES:

SCHWIENSCHLACT

Our Mennonite family working together to make the Mennonite Farmer Sausage and other Mennonite meat specialties.

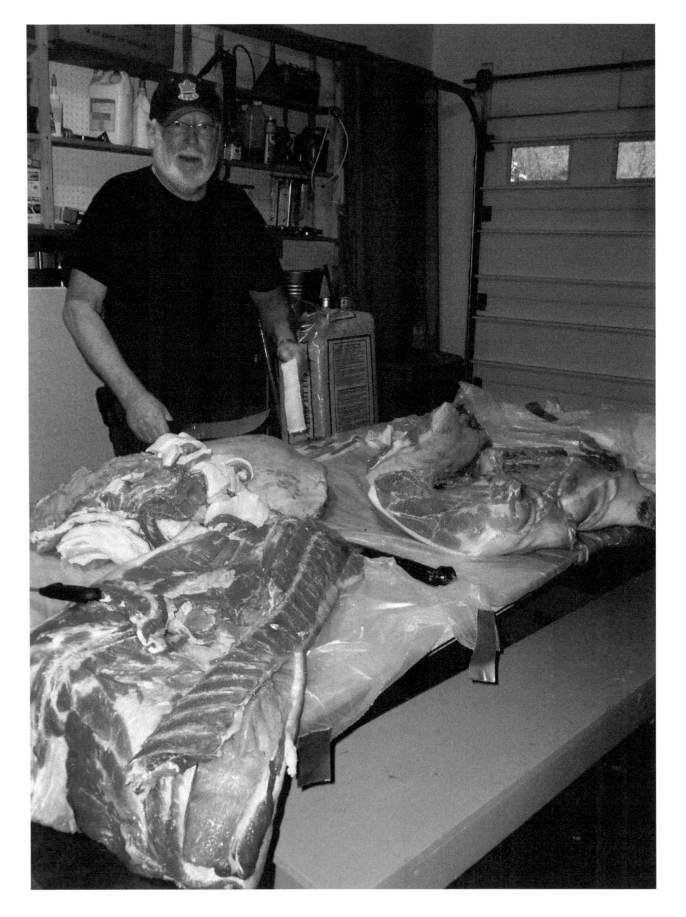

188

Featured here are the vintage meat stuffer for sausage and the vintage Meiagropa for making the Greiwa.

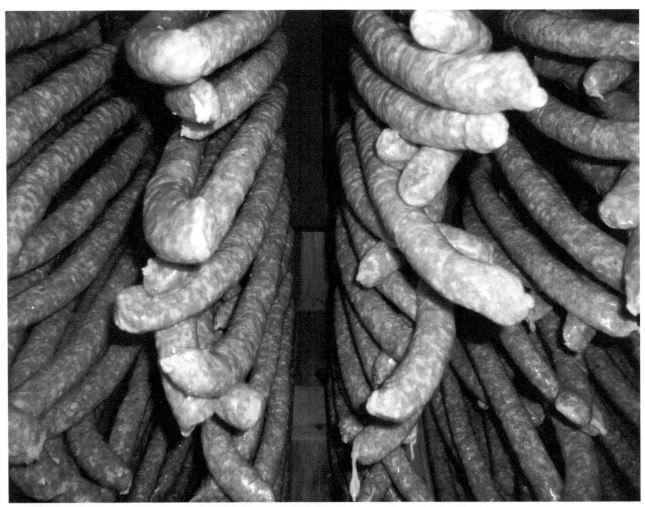

MENNONITE CRACKLES (GREIVA)

50 Lbs coarse ground pork fat

18 Pork jowls (whole)

This will make about 21 Lbs of crackles and about the same in rendered pork lard. Smaller batches can be made by reducing the portions of the meat in equal amounts of the fat and jowls.

To Prepare Pork Jowls:

Cut the jowls into 1 ½ inch strips, then carefully remove the skin from each strip. To remove the skin, have the jowl strip skin down and place a very sharp butcher knife at the edge between meat and skin. Slant the knife down close to the skin and pull the strip in a zigzag motion to separate the skin from meat. No skin should be left on the meat.

Coarse grind all the jowls in a meat grinder and mix together with the ground pork fat.

You will need:

30 Gallon Caldron (Meagroppa)

Or3 Gallon cast aluminum Pot

For large batch you will need at least a 30-gallon cast iron cauldron in an outdoor setting. You will also need a large wooden spoon paddle for stirring.

For the smaller batch you can use your outdoor BQ with the gas element using a 3-gallon large cast aluminum heavy pot. You will also need a large wooden spoon paddle for stirring.

To start:

Heat up the cauldron or the pot with a small amount of water in the bottom (about 5 cups for the cauldron) and (2 cups for the pot). When the pot and water are hot, add the ground meat mixture, at about a quarter at a time, start to stir the meat immediately. Do not let it stick to the bottom of the cauldron or pot. The whole success for making the crackles is the stirring, this will take about 3 hours of stirring and keeping the heat up and controlled. Stir to prevent any sticking to the bottom of the cauldron or pot until all the fat is rendered to a clear liquid and the meat crackles turn lightly brown. Turn the heat off at this stage and let the crackles settle down, if using a cauldron keep stirring and douse or remove the fire.

You will need lots of large crocks and heat proof pots for the lard and for the crackles.

Ladle as much as possible, of the clear liquid lard into clean heat proof crocks or large pots. Then in separate containers ladle the crackles also into clean crocks and large pots. Let stand in containers until the lard is mostly cool and solidified and until the crackles have cooled. Scoop the lard into freezer containers or Ziplock bags seal and freeze. Scoop the crackles into freezer containers or Ziplock bags seal and freeze.

How to Serve Crackles: To serve put the unthawed crackles into a small pot and heat until heated and bubbly. Remove from heat and drain through a sieve and press until all the fat is drained off. Return the crackles back into the pot add about 2 Tbsp. of water and heat and serve.

Serve with fresh bread, using small pieces of bread to pick up the crackles to eat with.

This is a great breakfast meal and very tasty.

This is a Traditional Mennonite Heritage recipe and made by all the Mennonites at a Hog Butchering and sausage and meat preparation gathering. These gatherings called a SCHWIENSHLACHT were held in November and into to early December, held by invite for family, neighbours and friends. This was a time when everybody worked together, and all the Mennonites took turns to help and prepare each other's meats, sausages and lard for the winter and into the spring. The hog butchering gathering started very early in the morning with first breakfast being served and lasted most of the day until all the work and clean-up was done.

MENNONITE SPARERIBS (REPSCHPEI)

This recipe has to be made with the crackles and pork fat together, in the cauldron as the crackles and fat are rendering.

You will need for the caldron: Less if using the pot.

 5- 8 Lbs Spareribs meat

Cut up the spareribs into pieces with 1 or 2 bones in each piece.

When the crackles and pork fat have rendered in the caldron for about 2 hours, place all the ribs into the caldron together with the hot rendering crackles and rendering fat.

Keep the fire up and keep rendering, stirring continuously for about another 1 ½ hours or so.

To test if the ribs are done the bone in the ribs should be loose and turn easily from the meat.

When all the ribs are done, using a large meat fork or a long-handled scoop remove and fish out all the ribs from the caldron.

Place the hot and cooked ribs into a large baking tray, salt lightly.

Set to cool and enjoy.

These ribs are like no other ribs you probably have ever tasted and worth the effort it takes to make them.

In a Mennonite home these would be served cold for breakfast.

This recipe is a Traditional Mennonite Heritage recipe.
This process of making these ribs, is the traditional process and is still used by John and Maria Klippenstein

PORK LARD (SCHMAULT AND GREIWA SCHMAULT)

BACON & SALTED PORK THE CURRING & SMOKING

1-10 lb. Pork belly (fresh and whole)
1 Cup pickling salt (coarse)
½ Cup black pepper (coarse ground)
The pork belly can be supplied by the butcher or a fresh meat wholesaler.
To Cure:
Cut the pork into half making them about 5 lbs each. Place the pork skin side down on a large and clean working surface. Than liberally using salt and pepper sprinkled over the meat, rubbing the meat to penetrate the salt and pepper. Place the meat skin side down into a cool dry place, such as a fridge. Let cure for about 12 - 24 hours.
The Meat Smoking:
2 Bags of Hickory wood smoking chips
2 Bags of Apple wood smoking chips
Take the slabs of meat and place a meat hook into a corner of the cured pork this is so that you can hang the meat into the smoke house. Hang the meat into the smoke house and then start your smoke.
You can use a large metal container such as a pail to start the smoke outside the smokehouse then place the smoking container into the smokehouse. Or you can start the smoke directly inside the smokehouse just making sure that no hot flame is started.
Keep the smoke going continuously for a full 4 hours and let the meat hang in the smokehouse until the next day or about 48 hrs.
Remove meat from the smokehouse trim and slice into 1 lb of bacon package and freeze. The trimmings make great salted pork for special dishes.

MENNONITE RUSSIAN HEADCHEESE
SILTFLEISCH

4 Pork Hocks
1 Small Garlic Bulb (peeled and chopped)
1 Tbsp. Black Peppercorns (crushed)
1 Tbsp. Red Pepper Chilli Flakes
3 Tbsp. Pickling Salt
2 Bay Leaves

Place the pork hocks into a large pot, cover the hocks under cold water until totally submerged by 2". Place all the other ingredients into pot with the hocks. Bring to a brisk boil then turn heat down to a very slow simmer. Simmer the meat for 2 ½ hours. Remove the meat into a glass9 x 12 baking dish. Let meat slightly cool then debone the meat while still quite warm and cut the meat and the skin into bit size small pieces. Discard all the bones but save all the juices the meat was boiled in. Evenly distribute the fine chopped meat in the glass dish and cover the chopped meat with enough juice to cover. Cool and set into the fridge to set for 12 hours or overnight.

To serve cut some small slices place in a plate cover with a small amount of vinegar, eat with a slice of bread.

LIVERWURST

3 Lbs. Pork liver (finely ground)
3 lbs. Pork (lean and finely ground)
3 Lbs Pork fat (finely ground)
2 ½Tbsp.s. black pepper
4 Tbsp. salt (coarse pickling salt)
1 Tbsp. white pepper

Mix all the ingredients together. Then stuff into 10" – 12" length casings, leaving enough casing at each so that they can be tied with kitchen string to form a ring.

Then place the sausages into a large pot of boiling water. Bring to a full boil and boil the sausages for 10 – 15 minutes. Then remove liverwursts from the boiling water and be careful not to puncher the skin.

Cool and can be frozen.

This is a Traditional Mennonite Heritage recipe
This recipe adapted by Maria Klippenstein

Original oil painting by Maria Klippenstein

MENNONITE COMMUNITY
HARVEST TIME & WORK BEES

Original oil painting by Maria Klippenstein

In a traditional Mennonite Heritage community, the Mennonite people would always work together.

They would help each other during harvest, field work, barn/home building, and with fall Schwiensclacht. Quilting was also a group project.

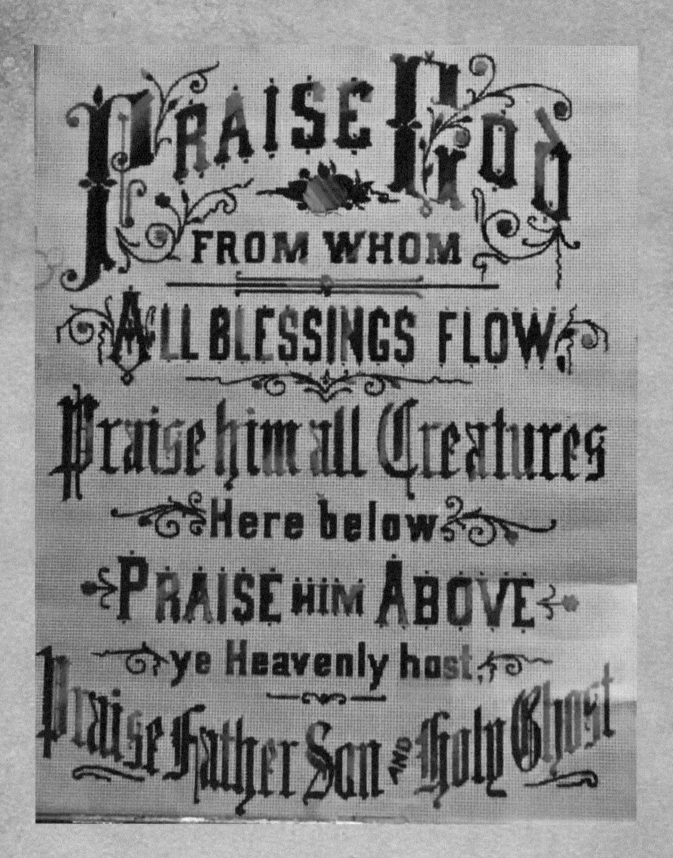

MENNONITE CHURCH & WORSHIP

The Chortitzer Mennonite Church in Southern Manitoba. This church was built in 1879 by the Chortitzer Mennonite that arrived from Russia in 1874. John, my husband and I were members and were married here. This picture is circa 1947 on a special celebration.

The interior of the Chortitzer Mennonite Church where special services were held.

The Chortitzer Mennonite Conference published a historical book circa 1874-1990.

Rev Henry G. and Maria Klippenstein
He was a preacher of the Chortitzer
Mennonite Church. She is dressed in
Mennonite style dress. circa 1929

Mr Abram and Louise Dueck
Mrs. Louise Dueck dressed in Mennonite
style dress and wearing a prayer cap. Circa
1930

Church shawl, Russian style

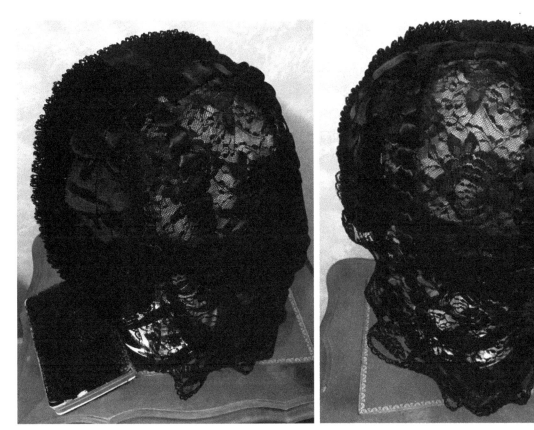

Prayer cap for Chortitzer Mennonite Church Services, typical Mennonite

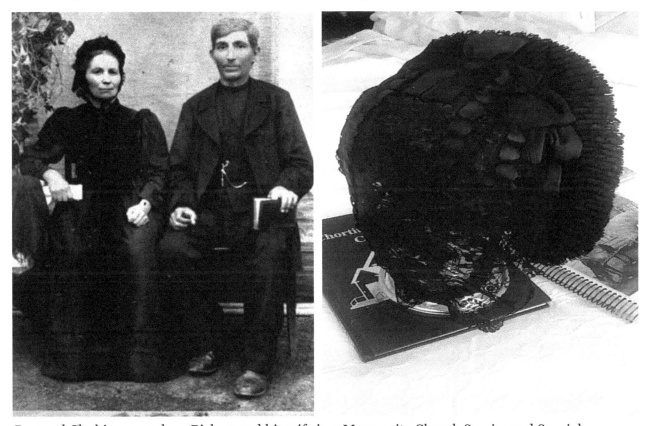

Pastoral Clothing worn by a Bishop and his wife in a Mennonite Church Service and Special Services. circa 1874 - 1935

Chortitzer Mennonite Church Women's Prayer Hat

Chortitzer Mennonite Church Communion Service
With Bishop Peter S. Wiebe and Reverend Abram F. Kehler
Oil Painting by artist Maria Klippenstein

Early Mennonite Dress and Prayer Hat
Mrs. Louise Deuck
Oil Painting by artist Maria Klippenstein

MENNONITE HOLY DAYS & HOLIDAY COSTUMS

Christmas (December 25): Christmas is Celebrated traditionally by going to a church service to honor the birth of Christ. Mennonites then will spend the day with family and extended family. More traditional Mennonites will also take time after Christmas, normally the 2 following to attend church services and family gatherings. Some families will set up a tree and decor, but some families disapprove, seeing these decorations as a pagan survival that has no place among Christians. To celebrate the morning of Christmas children would set out large bowls on Christmas eve, parents traditionally would place gifts in the bowls for their children to enjoy the next morning. Families would also take days off from work to travel and see family.

Epiphany (January 6): Mennonites would traditionally attend morning church services to commemorate the three wise men who came to visit Jesus. They would then spend the day visiting with family and friends.

Good Friday and Easter: Mennonites would attend church service on Good Friday and Easter Sunday. Good Friday is set apart as a day to reflect the death of Jesus Christ. Many traditional families will spend most of the day at home reflecting on the cost of Salvation and Jesus's willingness to die on the cross for all of us. On Easter Sunday the day is traditionally spent visiting family and having Easter egg hunts and goodie bags for the children. Same as Christmas holidays, some Mennonite families will welcome some more modern ideas connected to Easter, such as the Easter bunny, where others will not.

Ascension Day (the 6th Thursday after Easter): Mennonite families will attend church on this morning to honor the ascension of Jesus into heaven after done with his work on earth.

Pentecost (the 7th Sunday after Easter): Mennonites will attend morning church on this day commemorating the gift of the Holy Spirit to Christians and then will spend the afternoon gathering with family and friends.

OTHER DAYS OF INTEREST

Funerals: Commonly whole families will be seen in attendance at community funerals even when the person was not a relative.

Butchering: There are many Mennonite families that do their own butchering and processing of livestock. These skills are traditionally passed down from generation to generation, so children are often pulled from school to attend a butchering to learn this skill. Multiple families will sometimes get together and work as a team in a large butchering.

Halloween: Some Mennonites believe Halloween is Satan's day and they refrain from joining in any celebrations. Parents will discourage their children from taking part in any related activities. Being Christians, this can be a very sensitive issue for many Mennonites. Many deem Characters of Halloween such as witches and ghosts, as being associated to evil. Some Mennonite families will have an Autumn harvest party as an alternative!

Remembrance Day: Being from a non-resistant culture many conservative Mennonites disapproving of school activities regarding war or commemorating the military.

EASTER

Good Friday Maunday Thursday Communnion Service

A MENNONITE TRADITIONAL EASTER MEAL

A MENNONITE CHRISTMAS CELEBRATION

223

CHRISTMAS EVE CHILDRENS CHURCH CHRISTMAS PROGRAM

FOR UNTO YOU IS BORN THIS DAY IN THE CITY OF DAVID A SAVIOUR,
WHICH IS CHRIST THE LORD
"GLORY TO GOD IN THE HIGHEST,AND ON EARTH PEACE,
GOOD WILL TOWARD MEN."

The Christmas Eve Sunday School or Chidren Church program was a sacred celebration of the Christmas birth of Christ. It was presented to the church congregation and visitors by the children. Many hours were spent by the children to memorize their verses (fensh), song and bible scriptures to recite off by heart their part at the program. The children were dressed in their christmas clothes and hair was curled and neatly combed.
After the program had been presented and had concluded each child would receive a Lush that is a paper bag filled with candy,orange peanuts and other goodies

THE CHRISTMAS "LUSH "THE CANDY BAG

The candy, orange and peanut bag called "the lush " was given to each child after reciting their chrstmas verse and scripture. At the cristmas concert on cristmas eve.

THE CHILDREN CHRISTMAS GIFT PLATE

These plates were set out on christmas eve at home

THE FAMILY CHRISTMAS MEAL

ANCIENT MENNONITE CHRISTMAS HYMN"
DER FRIEDENSFUERST

Der Friedensfurst

Duet S&A

Uns ist ge-bor-en heut ein kind, Uns ist ge-bor-en heut ein sohn,

Und sei-ne Herr-lich-keit Full-et die wei-te Welt, Und er heiszt, und er heiszt

Wun-der-bar Wun-der-bar Der macht-ge Frie-dens-furst

Wun-der-bar Wun-der-bar Der macht-ge Frie-dens - -furst.

Drum be-

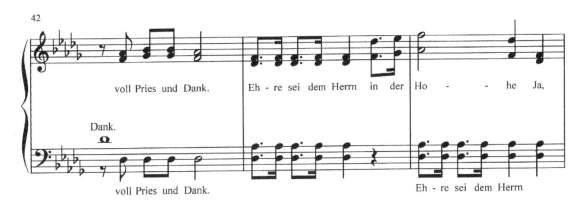

Eh - re sei dem Herrn in der Ho - - he Und Frie-de auf der wei-ten

Eh - re sei dem Herrn und Frie -de auf

D.S. al 𝄋

Welt, Gott-es Frie - de auf der Welt. Seid Froh-lich al - le

Der Wei-ten Welt

Vol-ker und sing - et Freu - den - lie-der, Bringt Eh - re und An - be-tung, ihm, dem

Frie - dens - furs - ten dar Singt Ho - si - an - na Ho - si -

Singt Ho - si - an - na

MENNONITE BOOKS, PLAUTDIETSCH LANGUAGE, WORSHIP & TEACHINGS

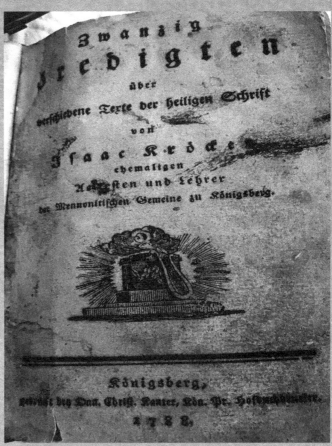

A Historical Mennonite book printed in 1788 in Koenigsberg. This book is the written word and consists of 20 Mennonite church sermons and teachings by Prediger Issack Krocker a Prediger and Teacher to the Mennonite Church of 1788 and earlier. This book is a family heirloom passed done to me and now belongs to the Maria Klippenstein Library.

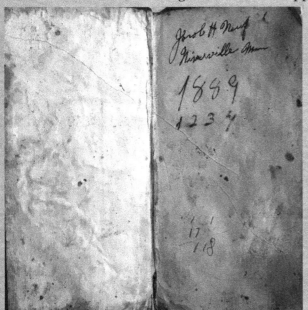

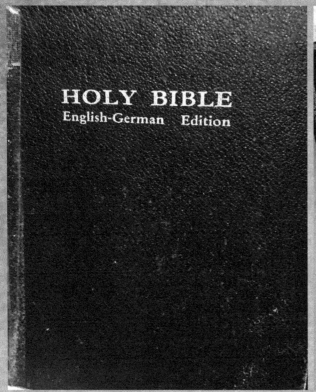

Above Photo: The Holy Bible in German and English. All knowledge for sermons and teachings was accumulated from the Holy Scriptures. The laws of Moses, 10 commandments, and the Teachings of Jesus Christ.. Love and Pacifism.

Above Photo: The Gesangbuch a 1912 edition of the songbook and accompanied by the Choralbuch a 1940 edition. These two books were used for the worship and chant singing in a Mennonite Church services and celebration. The Choralbuch had the song notes and melody for the men singers lead the church singing. (fehsinga)

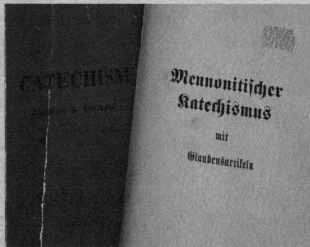

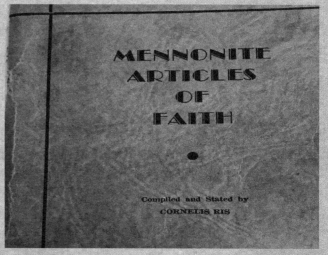

Above Photo: The Mennonite Church Catechism including the Mennonite Articles of Faith. German and English.
This Catechism was used as an instruction book in teaching the children and youth the Holy Scriptures. The book was in form of question and answer from the Holy Scriptures. Also, it had to be memorized in full, and was recited by the candidates at baptism. in order to become a church member

Above Photo: Mennonite Articles of Faith compiled by Cornelis Ris at Hoorn, Holland in 1747.

Deutsches Lesebuch used in the Mennonite schools to teach the German language and teach to write in the gothic German alphabet. The book was known as the Fibel

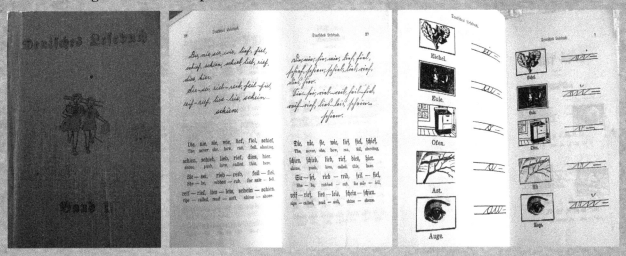

The Mennonite Plautdietsch and Low German language spoken in homes is lacking practise with the Mennonites. Also, the Plautdietsch is being neglected by the established
teaching Institutions for protecting this language and promoting training and knowledge of Plautdietsch.

THE WINDMILL TURNING

Nursery Rhymes, Maxims, and
Other Expressions of
Western Canadian Mennonites

VICTOR CARL FRIESEN

The Windmill Turning is a Plautdietsch child Nursery rhyme book that contains all the Mennonite rhymes and songs the Mennonite mothers and fathers would sing and say to their children.

The Architectural Mennonite Heritage

History of Mennonite Finance distribution Waisenamt

NOTES:

NOTES:

NOTES:

NOTES:

RECIPE INDEX

Lightning Source UK Ltd.
Milton Keynes UK
UKHW050922121219
355214UK00005B/42/P